# COMPOSITION WITH TWELVE NOTES

# Josef Rufer

# COMPOSITION WITH TWELVE NOTES
## related only to one another

*Translated by Humphrey Searle*

Barrie & Jenkins
London

ENGLISH TRANSLATION BY HUMPHREY SEARLE

COPYRIGHT 1954 BY
THE MACMILLAN CO. OF NEW YORK

SECOND IMPRESSION REVISED
1961 by Barrie & Rockliff (Barrie Books Ltd.)

THIRD IMPRESSION REVISED
1965 by Barrie & Rockliff (Barrie Books Ltd.)

FOURTH IMPRESSION REVISED
1969 by Barrie & Rockliff the Cresset Press

FIFTH IMPRESSION
1970 by Barrie & Jenkins Ltd.
2 Clement's Inn, London W.C.2

ISBN 0 214 65032 4

*Translated from the German Edition*
DIE KOMPOSITION MIT ZWÖLF TÖNEN

*first published by*
MAX HESSES VERLAG
*Berlin*, 1952

IN MEMORY OF
ARNOLD SCHOENBERG

PRINTED IN GREAT BRITAIN BY
LOWE AND BRYDONE (PRINTERS) LTD
LONDON

# TRANSLATOR'S PREFACE

JOSEF RUFER, who is at present lecturer at the Freie Universität, Berlin, on contemporary music and general musical theory, is a well-known international authority on modern music. He was Schoenberg's pupil and his assistant at the Prussian Academy of Arts in the 1920s; after Schoenberg's enforced departure for America in 1933 they nevertheless managed to remain in contact, in spite of the political difficulties of the time, right up to Schoenberg's death in 1951. Schoenberg had actually begun an active collaboration in this book, which may be regarded as the authoritative exposition of the Method of Composition with Twelve Notes, based on examples drawn from Schoenberg's own compositions as well as on his theoretical writings.

Rufer's book first appeared in Germany in 1952; twelve-note music, banned since 1933 in Germany and German-occupied countries, was now beginning to be written again there, but it had not gained a firm foothold either there or in the countries such as England, Sweden, Switzerland and the Americas where there had been no limitations on styles of composition. At first twelve-note composers based their style on Schoenberg's works: but, as Professor Walter Kolneder has said in his book on Webern, "the younger musicians soon showed a certain aversion, especially to Schoenberg's habits of expression. They quickly saw in the 'grand old man' of modern music a late Romantic burdened with the style of *art nouveau* and expressionism. . . . This aversion led to a critical attitude even to his technical methods of composition." However Kolneder was writing here of the avant-garde composers, especially those who frequented the annual Darmstadt Summer School, and in fact Schoenberg's reputation both as a composer and a theorist has grown steadily since his death. It is true that many of the younger generation have followed methods which derived in the first place from Webern rather than

Schoenberg, but Schoenberg's influence is still strong, even among the younger composers. Twelve-note technique is now part of the curriculum of practically every musical academy in the Western world, and in a good many Eastern countries too: nearly every young composer has been influenced by Schoenberg's methods, even if he uses them in his own individual way—which is in fact what Schoenberg wanted him to do. So that an exposition of "classical" twelve-note methods is still of importance, and is indeed essential for anyone who wishes to understand the development of music in this century.

Something needs to be said regarding the translation of the technical terms. It has been decided to speak throughout of "twelve notes" rather than "twelve tones"; the former is more accurate for English readers. However, Schoenberg himself, in his English articles written while living in America, naturally used the American term "twelve tones", and this has been retained in all quotations from Schoenberg himself.

The term *Grundgestalt* presented some difficulties. Some writers have equated this with the *Grundreihe*, i.e. the basic set or series of twelve notes (also known as tone-row or note-row) on which each twelve-note composition is based. However it is clear that Schoenberg used the term *Grundgestalt* (literally, basic shape) in a rather wider sense than this. Herr Rufer has clarified the point in a letter to me of 22 January, 1954, the relevant passage from which I give here:

In his composition teaching, Schoenberg formed the concept of the *Grundgestalt* (basic shape) as early as 1919 and used it with the exact meaning which it has in my book—as being the musical shape or phrase which is the *basis* of a work and is its "first creative thought" (to use Schoenberg's words). Everything else is derived from this—in music of all kinds, not only twelve-note music; and it is not derived merely from the basic *series* which is contained in the basic shape, but also from *all* the elements contained in the basic shape—that is to say, those elements which, together with the series as the melodic element, give it its actual shape, i.e. rhythm, phrasing, harmony, subsidiary parts, etc. In this connection it is especially important to note that Schoenberg, who in those days was working out his method for the first time, applied the results of his composition with twelve notes to composition in general from the outset, by choosing the concepts he used for the theoretical formulation of his method in such a way that they could also apply to music of any kind (tonal, classical, etc). This happened at a time when he was not yet *able* to teach twelve-note composition, as its formulation was not yet complete. And for this reason he did not need to teach twelve-note composition as a special subject later on, nor in fact did he ever do so: he only taught *Composition*, and it did not matter whether this was tonal, atonal, polytonal or anything else. In one of his articles which I saw after 1945 he mentioned himself that in his teaching of that period he quite consciously absorbed the newly-born perceptions drawn from twelve-note composition in analyses of Mozart, Beethoven and Brahms, but in a camouflaged form. In my very full notes of his teaching between 1919 and 1922 I find these definitions: a *motif* is the smallest musical form, consisting of at least one interval and one rhythm. The next sized form is the *Grundgestalt* or phrase, "as a rule 2 to 3 bars long" (the number of bars depending on the tempo, among other things), and consisting of the "firm connection of one or more motifs and their more or less varied repetitions". The next sized form, the *theme*, "arises from the need to connect several shapes together" and consists of "the connection (here he expressly does not say *firm*) of the *Grundgestalt* (basic shape) with its more or less varied repetitions".

It is quite clear from this that Schoenberg invented and used the term *Grundgestalt* as a concept which is *universally* valid in music, especially in analyses of classical music. So far as I know he never tried—as I have done with Beethoven's Op. 10, No. 1—to analyse a whole work showing its derivation from a *Grundgestalt*. But he certainly spoke of the possibility of doing this. I first decided to try it while working on my book, as an example, and had a startling success with the Op. 10, No. 1, at the first attempt, which is the most convincing proof one can possibly think of that Schoenberg's thesis was right—for it is a youthful work of Beethoven's, in which one can fairly safely exclude the possibility of construction of this kind being *conscious*. So it is called "basic shape" not only because it is a shape which contains the basic series, but also because it contains all the other elements which create musical shapes and is the starting-point of the musical development of the whole work. In tonal music the *key* takes the place of the *series*.

So *Grundreihe* (basic set or series) and *Grundgestalt* (basic shape) are two different things. The latter is a wide musical concept; the former belongs to twelve-note music and is a part of the latter. This must be brought out quite clearly, because in Schoenberg's music the *Grundgestalt* as the "first creative thought" is of primary importance, but not the series, which is derived from the *Grundgestalt*. On the other hand, for nearly all the twelve-note composers I know, the series is the primary element and starting-point! Both expressions, *Grundreihe* and *Grundgestalt*, come from Schoenberg himself."

I have therefore adopted the following terms: for *Grundgestalt*, "basic shape" (also used in Erwin Stein's *Orpheus in New Guises*);* for *Einfall*, which Herr Rufer in some passages equates with the *Grundgestalt*, I have used the term "conception" —though on occasions "inspiration" is made more suitable by the context; and for *Grundreihe*, "basic series". Schoenberg's own English term for this was "basic set," but "series" is perhaps better known to English readers and also enables one to speak of "serial composition" for *Reihenkomposition*.* For the German terms *Vordersatz* and *Nachsatz* (meaning the first and second phrases in a

* (Rockliff, London, 1953).

* In passages where the four different forms of the basic series are mentioned, I have used the terms "original series" (O), inversion (I), retrograde (R) and retrograde inversion (RI).

musical sentence) I have adopted the terms used by Schoenberg in his English writings—"antecedent" and "consequent".

I would like to express my thanks to Herr Rufer's daughter, Frau Iselin Hillel and to Mr. Peter Stadlen for the very considerable help they have given me in the preparation of this translation, which has deliberately been kept as close to the original as possible, and in which free paraphrase has generally been avoided.

H.S.

# CONTENTS

TRANSLATOR'S PREFACE . . . . . *page* vii

I SCHOENBERG'S METHOD OF "COMPOSITION WITH
TWELVE NOTES RELATED ONLY TO ONE ANOTHER"
AS PART OF THE GENERAL THEORY OF COMPOSI-
TION . . . . . . . . . 1
*Idea and technique (p. 2)—What is twelve-
note music? (p. 5)—Imagination, conscious and
unconscious construction (p. 7).*

II THE DEVELOPMENT OF TWELVE-NOTE MUSIC . 14
*Tonality's principle of organisation and its
formative function (p. 14)—Break-up of the
major-minor tonality (p. 15)—The trend towards
dodecaphony in music since 1900 (p. 16)—
"Twelve-tonality" as the result of an organic
development (p. 21).*

III THE ANTECEDENTS OF TWELVE-NOTE COMPOSI-
TION IN THE COMPOSITIONAL TECHNIQUE OF
CLASSICAL AND PRE-CLASSICAL (POLYPHONIC)
MUSIC . . . . . . . . . 24
*The principle of repetition and the principle of
variation as a means of creating shape and form
(p. 25)—the "connected antithesis" (p. 29)—
Basic "thematic" forms (p. 32)—Motivic working
and motivic variation (p. 37)—The basic shape
(Grundgestalt) and its pivotal importance in
musical exposition, development and the creation of
form, demonstrated in Beethoven's Sonata in C
minor, Op. 10, No. 1 (p. 38)—The parallel with
twelve-note composition (p. 45).*

IV  THE THEORETICAL AND MUSICAL BASES OF
SCHOENBERG'S COMPOSITION WITH TWELVE NOTES      46

*The emancipation of the dissonance (p. 47)—The
"Magic Square" (p. 48)—The "Musical Space"
(p. 49)—Synthesis of homophonic and polyphonic
development in Schoenberg's music (p. 51).*

V  SERIAL COMPOSITION IN SCHOENBERG'S OP. 23
AND 24 AS THE PRECURSOR OF COMPOSITION WITH
TWELVE NOTES . . . . . . .      55

*The basic conception (Grundgestalt) as a musical
law (p. 57)—The fields of force in music and their
changes (p. 57)—The melodic motif (p. 61)—The
basic shape as containing the musical thought
(p. 65)—The note-series as a melodic extract of
the basic shape (p. 63ff)—The Five Piano Pieces,
Op. 23, and the Serenade, Op. 24 (p. 61ff).*

VI  COMPOSITION WITH TWELVE NOTES. . .      79

I. *The derivation of a twelve-note series from the
basic shape (p. 80)—Essence and function of the
twelve-note series (p. 81)—The principle of the
intervals (p. 81)—The four forms of a twelve-
note series (p. 82)—The principle of the
co-ordination of the vertical and the horizontal
dimensions in music (p. 83).*

II. *The twelve-note series in practical composition.
1. Structure of a twelve-note series (p. 84).
2. Mirror forms (p. 84). 3. Use of the twelve-
note series or its notes in the horizontal and
vertical dimensions (p. 85). 4. Transpositions of
a twelve-note series (p. 86). 5. Change of octave
pitch—formation of complementary intervals
(p. 86). 6. Repetition of notes (p. 87). 7.
Avoidance of octave doubling (p. 90). 8. Subdivision of a twelve-note series—formation of
note-groups (p. 90). 9. The invention of a
twelve-note series (p. 91). 10. Alterations in*

*the twelve-note series (p. 94).* 11. *Corresponding intervals and note-groups (p. 97).* 12. *The interval-structure of the twelve-note series— specially constructed series (p. 100).* 13. *The meaning of the twelve-note series for composition—athematic music—the use of two different series—a new tonality (p. 105).* 14. *Typology of the twelve-note series—questions of notation (p. 111).*

VII    INVENTION AND VARIATION OF TWELVE-NOTE SERIES—THE FUNCTION OF RHYTHM.   .   .     112

     I *Melodic variations (p. 115)—The isorhythmic principle (p. 117).* 1. *Change of octave pitch (p. 115).* 2. *Mirror forms and transpositions (p. 116).* 3. *Distribution of a series between the vertical and horizontal dimensions (p. 119).* 4. *Exchange of note-groups (p. 122).*

     II *The creation and function of harmony in twelve-note music (p. 126).* 1. *Chord-formation through part-writing (p. 127).* 2. *Direct formation of chords from the twelve-note series (p. 128). Variations in harmony (p. 129). Tonal chord-formations (p. 130). The function of rhythm in twelve-note music (p. 131)—Connection of the repetitions of series—Choice of series (p. 132).*

VIII   THE INVENTION OF THEMATIC MATERIAL FROM A TWELVE-NOTE SERIES   .    .    .    .    .     135

     *The motivic character of the twelve-note series and the consequences of this for the technique of composition (p. 137)—The "motivic interval" and "motivic rhythm" as independent elements of a musical motif (p. 136ff)—The invention of various kinds of motivic material (p. 140)—Shown in the Fourth String Quartet, Op. 37 (p. 140)—The Ode to Napoleon, Op. 41 (p. 154)—The Fantasy for Violin and Piano, Op. 47 (p. 157)—The Three Songs, Op. 48 (p. 161).*

# CONTENTS

IX  MUSICAL FORMS IN TWELVE-NOTE MUSIC .  .  166
*Schoenberg's view of form (p. 168)—"Old" and new forms in Schoenberg's works (p. 169)— Attempt at an analysis of the Fantasy for Violin and Piano, Op. 47 (p. 173).*

Appendix  SCHOENBERG, SKETCH FOR A COMPOSITION COURSE .  .  .  .  .  .  .  177

CHRONOLOGICAL LIST OF THE MUSICAL WORKS OF SCHOENBERG .  .  .  .  .  .  .  .  180

TWENTY-ONE TABLES OF MUSICAL EXAMPLES
*between pages* 182 *and* 183

LIST OF SOURCES .  .  .  .  .  .  .  183

ACKNOWLEDGEMENTS  .  .  .  .  .  .  184

INDEX  .  .  .  .  .  .  .  .  .  185

## ILLUSTRATIONS

Arnold Schoenberg, 1944           *facing page* 10

Beginning of the 1st Psalm, Op. 50c        *Verso of above*

Facsimile of the series-table of the 1st Psalm        11

## CHAPTER I

SCHOENBERG'S METHOD OF "COMPOSITION WITH TWELVE
NOTES RELATED ONLY TO ONE ANOTHER" AS PART OF THE
GENERAL THEORY OF COMPOSITION

*Idea and technique—What is twelve-note music?—
Imagination, conscious and unconscious construction*

FOR some time after the appearance of the first twelve-note
works in the early 1920s, this kind of composition was confined
to a small circle of musicians centred on Arnold Schoenberg.
It is only since 1945 that more and more composers of all countries
and nationalities have begun to turn to it. This surprisingly
spontaneous development is probably due to the growing
realisation that Schoenberg's method of composition offered
a unified system controlling the raw material of music, which
since the beginning of the twentieth century had gradually and
organically emancipated itself from tonality—a system which,
lacking any arbitrariness or compromise, and yet preserving the
results of the development of non-tonal music, led from the state
of searching and experiment to a new path which also restored a
direct and creative link with the music of the classical and pre-
classical masters.

Moreover, it was soon realised that this method of composition
was of a general and fundamental significance which went beyond
the works of its creator; for it became clear that the individual
style of a composer was not in the least affected by it, and that it
could be used in an entirely personal manner, varied only by the
quality and degree of the creative imagination.

To-day these facts are so well known, especially to the younger
generation of composers—whether they realise it or not—and the
need for the practical knowledge and use of this method of com-

position is so great, that the time seems to have come to try and give an exposition of it, based on the music of Schoenberg. The need is all the more urgent since so little that is authentic seems to be known about his method and the idea that lies behind it. Consequently many vague and arbitrary notions are current which lead to misunderstandings and aid and abet misrepresentation, thus threatening to make Schoenberg's aims and ideas quite unrecognisable.

The plan of this book was conceived in the summer of 1949, and received the instant approval of the Master; however, its execution was delayed through external circumstances. Now his death has ended a collaboration which he had planned, and had, indeed, already begun. All the fundamental insights for which the author is indebted to Schoenberg, both directly and indirectly —especially from his long association with him as a pupil, and (from 1925 to 1933) as his assistant during Schoenberg's teaching activity at the Prussian Academy of Arts in Berlin—all these he wishes to record in this book, to the best of his knowledge and conscience, true to the purpose and spirit of this unique genius.

First of all, a warning: *Now as regards your plan of writing a book on twelve-tone composition. Do not call it Twelve-Tone Theory, call it "Composition with Twelve Tones". Personally, it is on the word Composition that I place the emphasis. Unfortunately most would-be followers of this method do something removed from the idea of composing music.*[1]*

These words outline the form and content of this book. Its task is the exposition of Schoenberg's method of composition and of its development as an organic part of the general theory of composition; by the exposition, firstly, of its fundamental idea and its theoretical and practical significance, secondly, of the form of the technique which Schoenberg himself developed on the basis of this idea in his own works.

This deliberately chosen sequence, Idea—Technique, should

---

* All quotations from Schoenberg are printed in italics. See numbered list of sources at the end of the book.

enable the student to develop from Schoenberg's idea an individual technique with complete artistic freedom, to suit his or her own imagination and musical language. The example of Schoenberg's own technique shows not only what freedom the musical imagination possesses within the laws of this self-discovered and self-imposed order; it also shows—and this is of especial importance—how great a part musical imagination can play in the actual use of the technique. To this we shall return later.

An idea is, so to speak, the *perpetuum mobile* of the mind; the creative spirit of man continually produces new manifestations of it. It is universally valid and, in contrast to its various concrete manifestations, remains general and non-individual. Anyone can re-think it at any time and give it a new and individual shape. This shape being the product of a personal process of thought and formation, also possesses individual characteristics, namely those of its creator. As soon as this process of thought and formation enters the realm of consciousness, it uses for the realisation of the "shape" a definite means of presentation—the technique. Technique, therefore, is an integral part of the individual process of thought and formation. The more individual and original the latter is, the more individual will be the technique which corresponds to it. *There is no technique without invention; on the other hand, it is possible to think of invention which has yet to create its technique.* Beethoven's technique is different from Brahms' or Schumann's or Bruckner's; Reger's modulations are as different from those of Schubert as Schubert's are from Mendelssohn's. For a genius, technique is a by-product of the creative imagination; technique which is mechanically adopted or imitated remains a recipe by which one can certainly "fabricate" music, but not "create" it.

This does not mean that the study of the theory of composition is superfluous or even harmful. At all times composers—even the great masters—learnt through study to express their musical thoughts more pointedly, fluently and clearly. In order to fulfil its rôle properly, the teaching of composition must keep two points in view. By abstracting general principles from the works of the great masters, it enables the average musical person with no special gift for composition to "compose" music, i.e. to put it together. This happens every day in musical academies, where the students write fugues, canons, rondos and so on. But there is one thing which the most conscientious pursuit of the study of composition cannot do—that is, replace inspiration, through which alone music becomes the immediate creative expression of thoughts.

That is the first consideration which an effective study of this kind must take into account. The second is this: any description and formulation of a technique is in danger of becoming dogmatic. This danger is all the greater since every beginner wants to be taught the "know-how" in the most exact and final manner possible. But a technique which lives up to expectations of this kind and replaces idea by dogma becomes rigid and is useless for genuine artistic creation. This would no longer be art and would have little to do with Schoenberg's lifelong aims and teachings: *The belief in technique as a saving grace must be discouraged, and the striving towards truthfulness encouraged.*[13]

Any useful method of teaching composition must therefore carefully balance the intellectual and the artistic. It must combine the two, if it is to give the artist what he needs: the greatest freedom within the strictest law. It is of necessity intellectual in the precise conceptual formulations which it abstracts from the great masterpieces. Without this intellectual precision it would be purposeless and useless. It must be artistic, in that it always remains conscious of its subservience to the idea, and, in a wider sense, to the creative imagination. For it is the work alone which justifies the means. Kant, in his *Critique of the Power of Judgment*, has said on this point: "Genius is the talent which gives art its rules".

Schoenberg has given rules to music, as it has developed in his hands and in the hands of many others since the beginning of the twentieth century. *Whether one calls oneself conservative or revolutionary, whether one composes in a conventional or progressive manner, whether one tries to imitate old styles or is destined to express new ideas—whether one is a good composer or not—one must be convinced of the infallibility of one's own fantasy and one must*

4

*believe in one's own inspiration. Nevertheless, the desire for a conscious control of the new means and forms will arise in every artist's mind; and he will wish to know consciously the laws and rules which govern the forms which he has conceived "as in a dream". Strongly convincing as the dream may have been, the conviction that the new sounds obey the laws of nature and of our manner of thinking—the conviction that order, logic, comprehensibility and form cannot be present without obedience to such laws—forces the composer along the road of exploration. He must find, if not laws or rules, at least ways to justify the dissonant character of these harmonies and their successions. After many unsuccessful attempts during a period of approximately twelve years, I laid the foundations for a new procedure in musical construction which seemed fitted to replace those structural differentiations provided formerly by tonal harmonies. I called this procedure "Method of Composing with Twelve Tones which are Related Only with One Another."* [2]

What is the music composed according to this method? What is twelve-note music? For the present the answer is quite short and simple: it is music like any other music. That is to say, it is good or bad music, depending on whether it comes from a good or a bad composer, from an imaginative and clear mind or from a poor and confused one, from one who knows his job or from a bungler. It is exactly the same as with all other music, whether it follows the principle of tonality or any other principle. For no one has yet claimed that the use of a major or minor key is a guarantee of good music.

Neither does composition according to Schoenberg's method give any such guarantee, nor is it a magic formula by which one can "calculate" music. For the idea and its realisation are, here as there, the indispensable prerequisite of artistic composition. If these are present, and if the structure of the musical idea is such as to exclude the use of tonality, then Schoenberg's "Method of composing with twelve notes which are related only with one another" certainly opens up *new possibilities of logical formal construction in the use of the twelve tones . . . for me the expression "logical" evokes these associations: Logic—human way of thinking*

5

*—human world—human music—human perception of natural law, and so forth.*[3] Schoenberg's method is therefore an artistic means of a pronouncedly *conservative* nature (to use the word in a wide sense) within the general field of composition. Its use prejudices the creative process no more than did the laws, rules and precepts of musical theory in previous times.

Bettina von Arnim told Prince Hermann von Pückler-Muskau about Beethoven's meeting with Goethe at Teplitz:

"Goethe visited him, and Beethoven played to him. When he saw that Goethe seemed to be deeply moved, Beethoven said: 'Sir, I did not expect this from you. Several years ago I gave a concert in Berlin; I had made a great effort, and thought that I had done well. I expected some decent applause, but when I had expressed my utmost enthusiasm, not the slightest sign of applause was forthcoming. That was really too much for me; I could not understand it. . . . But the riddle was solved when the whole Berlin public, being fashionably educated, staggered towards me with tear-sodden handkerchiefs to express their appreciation. To a crude enthusiast like myself this was quite irrelevant; I saw that I had a romantic but not an artistic audience. But to have this from you, Goethe, does not please me. . . . You must know yourself how stimulating it is to gain the applause of hands one respects. If you will not recognise me and regard me as your equal, who will? To what pack of ragamuffins must I play to be understood?' In this way he drove Goethe into a corner; at first Goethe could not think how he might undo the damage he had done, for he was well aware that Beethoven was right."

These words of Beethoven's, contrasting, as they do, the romantic and the artistic, pose a problem which runs like a pedal-point through all the many hundred years of the history of all the arts: what is the relative importance of feeling and intellect in art, and particularly in music? What is their relation, both in the creative process and in the finished work of art? Is creation a conscious or unconscious process? It is the question of the constructional element in a work of art.

Beethoven's words say quite unequivocally that he wished his music to be comprehended not by feeling alone, but also by the intellect; by that close combination of the two which he described as "artistic", and the achievement of which threw him into the "utmost enthusiasm". In other words, he wanted his artistic *labours*, the constructional content of his music, to be understood and appreciated. To understand this, we have only to study the sketch books of this master and see how he built up his themes and often remodelled them ten or more times before they satisfied him—not only in the domain of expression and feeling (where they remained essentially unaltered from the start), but with regard to their constructional functions in the work as a whole. Nothing is more revealing in this respect than the sketches for his String Quartet in C sharp minor, Op. 131, which are three times the length of the final score.

Music is an art of expression. This statement, however, is only correct if, while equating the concept "expression" with feeling (in association with the term *espressivo*), one also thinks of its wider function, of expressing something. One does not only express feelings, but also thoughts or visual images, not only in words, but also in notes, colours, plastic forms, etc. But: *There are relatively few people who are able to understand what music has to say purely through their musical faculties. The supposition that a piece of music must evoke images of some kind, and that if these are not forthcoming the work is unintelligible or worthless, is as widely believed as only false and banal ideas can be. One does not demand this of any other art, but remains content with the way its material affects us.*[4] (We shall have to concern ourselves later with the "way we are affected by the material" (i.e. the notes) of tonal as well as of twelve-note music, and also with its constitution, arrangement and constructional purpose.)

Feeling and intellect are both functions of human life. It would be absurd to deny their share both in the creation and in the appreciation of art. But we have to remember that the feelings of the creator and those of the listener—and again of each individual listener—differ very widely in kind and intensity, and that feeling cannot be taught, learnt or measured. It is the imponderable in a work of art. Therefore anything said about it and its rôle must be arbitrary and not universally applicable; it will therefore be meaningless.

Schoenberg answered the question "Feeling or Intellect?" by a reference to Balzac's philosophical story *Seraphita*, where it is said that the heart must lie within the domain of the head; and he developed the idea further: *It is not the heart alone which creates all that is beautiful, emotional, pathetic, affectionate and charming; nor is it the brain alone which is able to produce the well-constructed, the soundly organised, the logical, and the complicated. First, everything of supreme value in art must show heart as well as brain. Secondly, the real creative genius has no difficulty in controlling his feelings mentally; nor must the brain produce only the dry and unappealing while concentrating on correctness and logic. But one might become suspicious of the sincerity of works which incessantly exhibit their heart; which demand our pity; which invite us to dream with them of a vague and undefined beauty and of unfounded, baseless emotions; which exaggerate because of the absence of reliable yardsticks; whose simplicity is want, meagreness and dryness; whose sweetness is artificial and whose appeal attains only to the surface of the superficial. Such works only demonstrate the complete absence of a brain and show that this sentimentality has its origin in a very poor heart.*[5]

Even in daily life each one of us constructs; in conversation we unconsciously construct sentences. It is only through correctly constructed sentences that we can clearly express our thoughts and feelings (!), make ourselves understood or communicate. A poem, whether it deals with feelings or thoughts, is a *ne plus ultra* in artistic construction; what effort, arising out of the complications of rhyme and metre, must the poet, working in full consciousness, make in order to pour his thoughts and feelings into the form of the poem, carefully and deliberately choosing that form which will convey the meaning most clearly and intelligibly. The poet Hermann Hesse told a friend that for a fortnight he had done nothing but polish a four-verse poem in which the fourth line of the first verse had worried him. "And then I began to hammer it out seriously, line by line and word by word, and to test what was unnecessary and what was not. . . . At first the poem had four verses and now it only has three; I hope that it has become simpler and better as a result and has lost nothing essential."

Poetry and music are closely related through their common emotional components. Another poet of our time, Gottfried Benn, in his essay *Probleme der Lyrik* (Limes-Verlag, Wiesbaden) speaks of the fact that modern poets offer us what very nearly amounts to an out-and-out philosophy of composition, a system of creativeness. "Many of the general public think: 'there is a moor or a sunset, and there stands a young man or a young lady in a melancholy mood, and so a poem is born'. No, no poem is born like that. In any case a poem gets born very seldom—a poem is *made*. If you subtract the atmosphere from the rhymes, what remains, if anything remains at all, will perhaps be a poem." Anyone with a feeling for parallels will see the significance of this in the case of music, and will admit the importance of what Benn, with Nietzsche, calls "artistry" (*Artistik*)—"art as the real task of life, art as life's metaphysical activity"—which he regards as a characteristic of modern poetry, as opposed to the "emotional, subjective and thematic-melodious". Artistry, which we immediately associate with "art for art's sake"—a creed to which Schoenberg adhered without reservations—artistry, according to Benn, is not a popular expression in Germany. "It is, however, an extremely serious and pivotal conception. Artistry is art's endeavour, within the general dissolution of contents, to experience itself as a content, and from this experience to create a new style; it is the endeavour to set a new transcendence against the general breaking-down of values—the transcendence of creative stimulus. . . . Critics cannot rid themselves of the idea that a poem deals with feelings and should spread warmth—as if a thought were not a feeling, and as if form were not the supreme manifestation of warmth." And here we reach the crux of the matter. For what is

9

the meaning of the term "constructed music"? To reject this concept on emotional grounds is to disregard the most decisive fact, that an artist is a person with a strong imagination. If he constructs something he can never keep imagination out of it—in other words, he will always construct imaginatively. But, when confronted with music which was created in this way, who can differentiate or evaluate what is to be ascribed to intellect and what to feeling? Or, putting it differently, what is constructed consciously and what unconsciously? If construction is seen in this context of the un- (or sub-) conscious, even predominantly emotional people could not find anything here that would be incompatible with the concept of "Art". For then construction merely means starting off from a creative vision of the whole, as the artist sees the work before him in his mind, and presenting a group of thoughts in such a way as to reflect and express the idea of this whole; constructing, in fact, means to connect our thoughts according to our laws of human thought and feeling—laws which regulate our conscious as well as our subconscious being, for they are the laws of both our intellect and our heart. Both intellect and heart function logically in the truest sense of the word; i.e. they are capable of sensing and recognising connections, even if these connections are not obvious.

An idea is creative if it says something to us which has not been said before, at least not in this form, or if it shows up connections between something already known and something new (by "constructing" them into a unity), so that they are recognised and expressed in this way for the first time. In the case of such a truly creative idea it is of no importance whether it has come into being wholly, partly, or not at all as a result of conscious construction, or whether the process of making the separate parts of the idea into something new by integrating them, instead of merely *adding* them together, has taken place in the subconscious. Tonality itself is merely the result of certain principles of construction. One such principle, for instance, regulates the building of chords in thirds and defines their harmonic values. It connects them, on the basis of various established root-progres-

Arnold Schoenberg (1874-1951)
(*Private photo*, 1944)

Beginning of the 1st Psalm Op. 50 C (O Du mein Gott: alle Völker preisen Dich und versichern Dich ihrer Ergebenheit—O Thou my God; all the peoples praise Thee and assure Thee of their devotion). The text was written on 29 September 1950; the composition was begun at the end of 1950, and breaks off in the 86th bar, at the words "und trotzdem bete ich—and yet I pray".

Schoenberg planned to write a series of ten psalms to his own texts; the texts of nine were completed, but the tenth was left unfinished. The 1st Psalm, Schoenberg's last work, is written for speaker, mixed chorus and orchestra.

Facsimile of the series-table of the 1st Psalm

sions, in chord-sequences with quite definite functions and quite definite effects, like cadences, modulations, and so on. Whenever one wanted to achieve these effects one had to know and use the constructional laws and rules of tonality—consciously or unconsciously.

The same applies to music which employs constructional principles which can *only* be used consciously, those of double and multiple counterpoint: the so-called mirror-forms—i.e. inversion, retrograde and retrograde inversion of a theme—augmentation and diminution of themes, and other consciously constructed forms like canon and fugue. A fugue subject had to be invented in the so-called stretto, i.e. in double or multiple imitation of itself. It was therefore necessary to construct the theme with care, that is to say, to keep on altering it until it would obey the many rules of contrapuntal writing. And within the fugue itself the subject had to be answered according to quite definite constructional rules in the so-called Hexachord, in order to ensure that its intervals were exactly the same when transposed on to different degrees of the scale. This principle of interval-identity, not only in name but also in actual size—a principle which is so characteristic and essential in polyphonic music—will also be found in twelve-note music. Only when the fugue subject fulfilled all these constructional conditions did it become music in the form of the fugue. Bach's "Well-Tempered Clavier," "Art of Fugue" and "Musical Offering" are full of the boldest sound-constructions of this kind. Hence we can understand Willibald Gurlitt's remark that Bach's originality and mastery "lie less in his gift of good musical ideas and in the quality of the musical invention (*inventio*) than in a power of creative combination by which the traditional subjects, having been moulded by others beforehand, are developed, worked out and elaborated".*

* *Durchgeführt* (literally, "led through"). The usual German term for the development section in a sonata movement is *Durchführung*, implying that the thematic material of the exposition is here *led through* various regions which contrast with the main tonality of the movement. Schoenberg (*Structural Functions of Harmony*, p.145) therefore rejected "development", "working out" or "elaboration" as correct translations of *Durchführung*, and could not find a really satisfactory English equivalent. H.S.

So one might say that the composer first gets the thematic material ready, forms and tests it, consciously evaluating it in his imagination with regard to its carrying capacity and universal usefulness—so that he can then go ahead unhaltingly with the building of his work, which in his mind he sees throughout as a whole and as an *a priori* "Idea". Now he can be certain that the formal elements constructed in this way and prepared and "sized" to the last degree, will be able to support the boldest flights of his imagination.

Schoenberg found an ingenious example of thematic construction in Beethoven's String Quartet in F major, Op. 135, maintaining that it did not matter in the least whether this had arisen consciously or unconsciously:

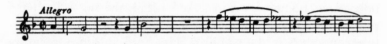

He looked for a thematic connection between the four-bar antecedent (first phrase) and the consequent (second phrase) of the theme, and finally discovered the following relation, which is both complex and unmistakable:

The consequent consists of the retrograde inversion of the antecedent, i.e. of its motif, the three notes of which are linked by the scale notes between them. Thus the whole theme is constructed out of a single motif. To sum up: constructive imagination and imaginative construction both have their necessary and, on occasion, complementary share in composition.

Schoenberg indicated the natural order of the two when he said that *invented principles of construction are always less important than those which are discovered unconsciously. If more happens than one can think out, this can only happen in the subconscious.*[6] Certainly the profounder and artistically more valuable inventions are the sole property of the subconscious. This is what Schoenberg means when he says that *the capacity to fulfil instinctively and unconsciously the demands of constructive lawfulness in music should be considered the natural condition of a talent.*[2]

## CHAPTER II

# THE DEVELOPMENT OF TWELVE-NOTE MUSIC

*Tonality's principle of organisation and its formative function—Break-up of the major-minor tonality—The trend towards dodecaphony in music since 1900—"Twelve-tonality" as the result of an organic development*

MUSIC is a kind of language. *It expresses the unconscious nature of this and other worlds.*[6] Just as music itself has widened its field of expression in the course of the centuries, keeping pace with the spiritual evolution of humanity, so its forms of expression and its grammar, following the needs of composition, have kept in step with this development. This organic evolutionary process has naturally also included the material of music, the notes themselves. As this material remains only a means to the end of providing musical sense, it had of necessity to take its structure and principles of organisation from music alone. The logic and laws of artistic experience and of the conditions of artistic development also influenced the structural organisation of musical material—by way of ensuring the greatest sensibility and homogeneity which could possibly come from the material itself in order to meet the play of musical imagination and its individual flavour.

Notes have no recognisable relation to objective and apprehensible things, just as a colour cannot express precise meaning. Notes only acquire meaning—naturally a purely musical one—from the way they are handled and connected with one another—for instance, if two or three are joined together in a motif, or more of them into a melodic or thematic shape. Although this meaning is purely musical it completely corresponds to human thought and feeling, and is identical with it; the fact that music emanates from man proves this identity, which at the same time is a prerequisite for its comprehensibility. For a human being can only behave in accordance with the degree of his development.

One of the most important means of defining the musical material is tonality. The first creates the conditions necessary for its most important function, that of building forms, by subjecting the twelve notes of our tempered system to a constructional organisation which is appropriate to the material and may be compared with a process of magnetism; the magnet is the key-note, which forces all the other eleven notes into relationship with itself. In the horizontal dimension it arranges seven of the twelve—leading away from and back to itself—in a fixed series of intervals which we call the major and minor scales. The remaining five notes are set in the intervals between the others, and may be used instead of the notes which are their immediate neighbours, in the sense of a change of colour (chroma). In the vertical dimension the key-note arranges the same twelve notes in chords whose different tonal value can be assessed, and whose construction by intervals of thirds is partly natural (derived from the harmonic series) and partly artificial (tonic to minor third).*

So the texture of music is already, as it were, infiltrated by tonality in all dimensions *ab ovo*, from the nature of the material itself. The way in which this happens produces that close connection and co-ordination between melodic and harmonic phenomena which exist in every true work of art and are both the precondition and the characteristic of the creation of musical form. We must take special note of this connection and correspondence between the harmonic and the melodic elements in tonal music, because its rôle in Schoenberg's method of composition with twelve notes is of similar importance.

Thus the constructional importance of the key-note consisted in the fact that it regulated the sequence of the notes in both the horizontal and the vertical dimensions, melodically as well as harmonically. From this organisation of the material tonality was

* Goethe had already remarked on this important structural distinction in a letter to Zelter.

able to develop its powers of creating form, thriving on it as on a seed-bed. Naturally this was the case only so long as the creative imagination of the composer accepted this order of things. In the last hundred years, and even more since Wagner, the development of music led gradually (and for a long time without anyone becoming aware of it) to a progressive weakening of tonality and its functions, through the infiltration of chromaticism. This led, both harmonically and melodically, to new interval-relationships between the twelve notes, which made it increasingly difficult to relate them to a key-note, and demanded more and more complicated means for the maintenance of the tonal structure. Thus the unifying effect of the key-note, the defining centre to which everything was related, which held everything together and kept it in formal balance, was gradually weakened. In this way one of the strongest foundations of music hitherto became more and more brittle. So arose the conception of enlarged, and finally of suspended, tonality. The harmonic style of impressionism, such as Debussy's, had indeed often preserved the aesthetic effect of tonality, but in practice had already abandoned its constructional function. Here a major or minor chord still represented the aural effect of tonality, but beneath the surface of the sound, so to speak, no constructional purpose remained. The latter had disappeared through the dissolution of tonality and the lack of tonal relationships in the chord-sequences of the impressionists. As mentioned above, this was an unconscious and necessary development, subject only to the logic of the creative imagination. Finally, in the first decade of this century, it led to the threshold of non-tonal music.

At this point it is interesting (and also important for the understanding of the trend towards twelve-note music) to follow the process of the dissolution of tonality as reflected in musical works, especially since 1900, and to discover the forces which played a part in it. Remembering how in the field of biology everything which dies contains the seed of a new life, one could expect to be able to see the signs of a new organisation and the beginnings of a new order appropriate to the material in the progressive alteration of the musical structure which arose through the cessation of tonal definition.

When one talks of non-tonal music, one thinks first and chiefly of the sphere of harmony. But here the process of dissolution had set in first and most strongly, and had already brought about such a fluid situation that it was hardly possible to find an actual point from which to start such investigations. It was different in the sphere of melody, the development in the horizontal dimension. In tonal music melody too was naturally defined and fixed by tonality; here scales and triads represented the organisation of our tempered (N.B. therefore artificial!) system of music. The entire thematic and melodic material of tonal music consists of scale-fragments, and of tonal intervals and broken triads—and sometimes of combinations of both.

Naturally the process of dissolution also seized on these melodic elements in music. The results of this we shall now show, quoting themes by notable contemporary composers of the first two decades of the twentieth century.

The music of Richard Strauss carried this process of the dissolution of tonality a decisive step forward, especially in "Salome" and "Elektra." But already long before this, in the symphonic poem "Also sprach Zarathustra," the following theme can be found:

It contains all the twelve notes in a self-contained form, without repetition. The end of this work, a B major chord over the bass note C, a model example of suspended tonality (which was received with horror and head-shakings by the professional musicians of the period), derives its organic meaning from this theme. But even in the opera "Arabella," in which the composer had again come to terms with the problems of modern music, the following twelve-note melody can be found in the first act (piano score p. 22, Langsames Walzertempo).

Nine of the twelve notes appear as principals. The chromatic phrase leading up to each of them and the accompanying harmonies make a definition of tonality difficult or impossible.

In the later works of Max Reger a quantity of 9-, 10-, 11-, and 12-note themes and phrases can be found.

Reger, String Quartet in F sharp minor, Op. 121, first movement, nine bars after figure 1.

This five-bar melodic shape contains (without repetition as defined by Schoenberg's method)* ten of the twelve notes; the eleventh and twelfth, G and B, appear at the same time as the tenth to make up the final chord. In the Violin Sonata, Op. 122, the following eleven-note phrase can be found; the missing twelfth note comes right at the beginning in the bass.

* See p. 87.

In the String Trio, Op. 141b, the main theme of the first movement is a twelve-note one; five notes—C, C sharp, D, G and B flat—are repeated within the theme.

Similar melodic forms containing many different notes can be found in the early works of Paul Hindemith. The third movement of his second String Trio begins with a two-bar basic shape of ten notes. The eleventh and twelfth, D sharp and G, appear in the first bar in the 'cello and viola.

The introduction to the opera "Cardillac" begins with an eleven-note phrase,

while the passacaglia theme in the third act shows the following arrangement of the twelve notes:

The fugato theme with which Hindemith's third String Quartet begins contains **ten** of the twelve notes (here with repetitions) in a four-bar phrase. But it is interesting that the fugal entry of the viola which follows begins with the eleventh note, F.

The first String Quartet of Béla Bartók contains this twelve-note theme:

The same trend towards dodecaphony in relation to melody can naturally also be found in the early tonal works of Schoenberg, Webern and Berg, as well as in their non-tonal compositions up to about 1920. The opera "Wozzeck" is particularly revealing in this respect.

Now compare these themes with the tonally organised themes of classical music, with their broken triads and scale fragments; notice the many intervals foreign to the key, and it will become apparent that, in melodic development too, the exclusive and compelling relationship to a key-note or tonality was disappearing all the time. All these examples (which could be multiplied at will both from the composers mentioned above and from others) show, in spite of all varieties of style, the same unconscious tendency, arrived at simultaneously and independently, to use as many as possible of the twelve notes within a narrow space when building melodies and themes; and, to some extent, not to repeat one note before the other eleven have been heard. The fact that this melodic development happened unconsciously clearly proves that twelve-note ideas can arise from the creative imagination without further ado, and are in no way limited to conscious construction. This shows how right Schoenberg was when he said, in a lecture at the University of California in November,

1949, that he did not create the twelve-note method; it was there to be discovered, it simply *had* to be discovered, and he was only surprised that other composers also had not recognised this necessity.

So the imagination of all these composers—and this is shown by the melodic development of their music—intuitively worked in the same direction and in the same way. They obeyed a law which was present, though not yet formulated or openly pronounced; it was to Schoenberg that its power of creating order and unity revealed itself. His creative imagination, more logical and consistent than that of other composers, had given up the controlling principle of tonality (which had become less and less powerful) and led the development of music into unknown paths. But at the same time his feeling for form led him to sense the necessity of a new order and means of control capable of consciously evaluating the new methods and forms, and the new rules and laws which governed these forms. As a musician, he could only seek and find these in his actual works, which through a natural organic development had reached and finally crossed the frontiers of tonality. From now on his music had lost one important element of the creation and maintenance of form, i.e. tonality. At the same time the tonal organisation of the twelve notes—as represented by triads and scales—no longer applied. On the other hand, if non-tonal music was the result of an organic and truly creative development—and this is borne out by the works written over a period of decades by many composers who were uninfluenced by one another and who all intuitively developed along similar lines—then it too must have a fundamental idea and law; and this law would have to be capable of establishing order within the raw material of music, i.e. within the twelve notes, just as the major-minor tonality did.

Schoenberg the musician found the root of this new order in the basic musical *conception* of a work. Whether one calls this a theme, melody, group of motifs or anything else, in tonal music it contained all the ingredients of the work in question—key, character, possibilities of exposition and development. Similarly, in the new, musically purposive organisation of sound, everything had to follow from and arise out of the idea, the basic conception. Just as in a tonal conception the notes are combined vertically in triads and horizontally in broken chords and scale fragments, in intervals and sequences of notes forming a group which is moulded into motifs and varied in character, so we can see a new characteristic of melodic creation in the tendency towards twelve-note writing. The sequences of notes and intervals, which are born of the basic musical conception and defined by it, form, both in tonal and in twelve-tonal music, the natural means of expression and the new order which governs the whole work. This was a decisive discovery of a new system of laws in non-tonal music.

The sequences of notes and intervals in a basic conception which tends towards twelve-tonality—legitimised in this, as we have seen, by the imagination of the most differing composers—form a note-series, which, in association with the usual thematic and formal development of classical and pre-classical music and their various means of expression, controls the order of the notes in a way similar to that of tonality—following the law of the original idea, which is the fundamental basis of the creation of the note-series.*

It follows from what has been said so far that the development of composition with twelve notes neither arises from intellectual

---

* In a letter to Nicolas Slonimsky (*Music Since 1900*, New York, 1938, p. 574) Schoenberg described the development of his composition with twelve notes: "The 'Method of composing with twelve tones' had had many 'first steps' (*Vorversuche*). The first step was taken about December, 1914, or at the beginning of 1915, when I sketched a symphony, the last part of which later became the 'Jakobsleiter', but which has never been continued. The Scherzo of this symphony was based on a theme consisting of the twelve tones. But this was only one of the themes. I was still far away from the idea of using such a basic theme as a unifying means for a whole work. After that I was always occupied with the aim of basing the structure of my music *consciously* on a unifying idea, which produced not only all the other ideas but also regulated their accompaniment and the chords, the 'harmonies'. There were many attempts to achieve this, but very little of it was finished or published. Suddenly I became conscious of the real purpose of my efforts; it was unity and order which had led me this way unconsciously. It was neither a straight way, nor did it arise through mannerism, as often happens with revolutions in art. Personally I hate being called a revolutionary, which I am not. What I did was neither revolution nor anarchy. I have always possessed a strongly developed feeling for form and a great aversion to exaggerations. With me nothing comes under a law, because nothing was ever unlawful; on the contrary, it is an ascent to a higher and better order." (3 June, 1937).

experiment, nor is it an arbitrary act of any kind; it is merely the translation into sound of a perception formed by the imagination of a musician and its natural consequences. All Schoenberg has done is to recognise the alteration in structure, which emerged in the most creatively important fields of music after 1900, as a purposive organic process within the general development of music, to show its significance theoretically and to formulate it. The decisive point—which is where his genius lies—is that the summing-up of this in the form of the Method of Composition with Twelve Notes in fact brings tradition and new elements together in a mutually fruitful synthesis; on the other hand it provides all possible scope for individual interpretation and use, and thus also provides that freedom of creative imagination, whose sole task is to make music. For *This method may be followed strictly, but handled freely.*[6]

Through the course of the evolutionary development of music, and as a result of the alterations in structure connected with this, the organising principle of tonality as an arbiter of form finally ceased to be adequate. In its place there appeared, as the bearer of a new tonality, the twelve-note series—if one understands the concept of tonality in the sense of a general principle of organisation. This new tonality, like the major-minor tonality before it, is combined with all the other means of composition which have been developed in classical and pre-classical music in Composition with Twelve Notes.

## CHAPTER III

THE ANTECEDENTS OF TWELVE-NOTE MUSIC IN THE
COMPOSITIONAL TECHNIQUE OF CLASSICAL AND PRE-CLASSICAL
(POLYPHONIC) MUSIC

*The principle of repetition and the principle of
variation as a means of creating shape and form—
The "connected antithesis"—Basic "thematic" forms
—Motivic working and motivic variation—The
basic shape ("Grundgestalt") and its pivotal
importance in musical exposition, development and
the creation of form, demonstrated in Beethoven's
Sonata in C minor, Op. 10, No. 1—The parallel
with twelve-note composition*

QUOTING both Beethoven and Schoenberg, we may regard
a piece of music as a kind of message from a musical poet or
thinker. The content of such a message consists of the assembling
of a series of musical thoughts into a unity, and establishing
relationships between them. The fundamental idea of the piece
explains itself in the coherent presentation of these thoughts.

In order to communicate themselves, these abstract thoughts
must assume a concrete motivic, thematic or melodic *shape*. In
order to gather its characteristic features firmly together, such a
shape needs a form—i.e. it needs definition and subdivision.
Thus we speak of small "thematic" forms, which in turn develop
into larger forms like Scherzo, Rondo and so on. All these events
take place, as it were, in the various concentric circles which
(like the skins of an onion) together make up a sphere; the centre
of the sphere would then represent the all-embracing idea of the
piece, and this is reflected in the various concentric circles.

In the course of the last few centuries some fundamental

principles of the presentation of musical thoughts in shapes and forms have developed in Western music. These principles have played such a decisive part, both in the creation of the smaller "thematic" forms and in the development of larger movement-forms out of these, that one can describe them as the antecedents of every kind of form-building. It is convenient that one can thus give a unified presentation of the concept of form, without regard to the stylistic changes which music has undergone in the course of time.

In order to communicate thoughts clearly and intelligibly, one has to find a form suitable for the purpose. Therefore form is necessary in music, in order to communicate a content and to act as a medium. Form depends on (a) the content and (b) the kind of presentation employed. The characteristic features of form are definition and subdivision. Ideally, therefore, form is never an end in itself, but only a means to the end of communicating musical thought and its development. The two principles which play the chief part in the creation of a musical form are repetition and variation. Repetition is the primary stage; variation and development are the higher stages in the evolution of compositional technique.

Only things which belong together and possess affinity can cohere, that is, become a form. In music, repetition is the seed-bed in which this coherence is developed. Repetitions of the smallest formal element, the motif, have a unifying effect, and ensure that all parts of a work can be related to one another and thus create the necessary conditions for the building of its form. Music is unthinkable without repetition.

But repetition has yet another function, which was probably its original one, and which only later led to the creation of form. In order to grasp something it is necessary to be able to remember it. In fairly complicated music repetition is necessary for the sake of comprehensibility. One must repeat the subject matter many times; this is no doubt the reason for the repetition marks in the older music. Primitive forms like dances and folk-songs particularly need repetition. Here it is necessary to be simple all the time and also to repeat the simple things often, for this kind of music aims to speak to everyone, and so must adapt itself to the comprehension of the most primitive.

However exact and unvaried repetition would not only be monotonous, but it would only permit an arbitrary ending of the music, not a proper conclusion achieved by a natural organic limit (a parallel is the Greek Meander pattern, whose exactly repeated motivic design of lines allows only of cessation, but not of conclusion); and as limitation is a characteristic feature of form, exact, unvaried repetition cannot, therefore, build forms. For every form grows towards a conclusion, a limit, while simple cessation is characteristic of something unformed. One of the most striking differences between good and bad music is that the former comes to a conclusion, while the latter just ceases. Therefore, for a higher level of form-creation, the principle of repetition must be allied to the principle of variation. Both are already discernible in the smallest unit of musical form, the motif. This consists of at least one characteristic interval and one characteristic rhythm, and is recognisable through being repeated many times; in this repetition the motif may either be altered or may remain unchanged.

As we have said above, the simplest forms contain primitive, i.e. frequent and hardly varied, repetitions. In art-forms repetitions of motifs are varied in proportion to their formal functions, and thus contribute to the development of the work. Further, variation helps to avoid or conceal any monotony that might be created by repetition, thus ensuring a richer and more varied flow of the music. Repetition combined with variation allows the unit to create the manifold by procreating new shapes through "developing variation". In contrast to this, mere varying of the figuration leaves the main part (which is where the "development" takes place) completely unaltered, and only affects the harmony, accompaniment and subsidiary parts.

In parenthesis; we can thus see that tonality is by no means the only artistic method of producing a unifying effect. Much the same applies to the capacity of tonality for creating tension, a capacity which music allegedly lost when tonality was relinquished. If we study the music of the nineteenth century from this angle, we find that other means besides tonality have the power of creating forms and tensions. But these forces were so closely associated with tonality that they were practically assimilated by it, and played no independent part of their own. Now, after the elimination of tonality, the higher demands made on these forces brought about their regeneration—certainly a positive result of the destruction of tonality. One can clearly see from any Beethoven sonata that the elements of tension in tonal music are not produced merely by the harmonic scheme, but arise at least equally strongly from the opposition of contrasting ideas and themes, and from the varying "density" of the different sections. After all, in a work of art which is shaped as a unity, how could an effect be due to only one of its components? Could the others have no part in it at all? Clearly tension always arises from the whole structure, i.e. melody plus harmony plus rhythm, the harmonic scheme being only one component. In non-tonal music, where this scheme is absent, its function of creating tension has been taken over by rhythm which, robbed of its stronger partner, tonality, has rapidly developed its share in the shaping of music, and correspondingly increased its elasticity and sensitivity. This reminds one of the phenomenon frequent in biology, where the disappearance of one element is so often followed by the increased activity of another, or even by an entirely new appearance.

Variation of a motif can occur (a) in the interval (b) in the rhythm and (c) in both.

(a) Beethoven, Symphony No. 5:

(b)

From the motif is developed, by means of repetition plus variation, the "shape" (*Gestalt*) or phrase. Usually this contains two to four bars (or multiples of this in quick tempi) and consists of the firm connection of one or more motifs with their repetitions in a more or less varied form.

(a) Beethoven, Sonata Op. 2, No. 3, first movement.

(b) Beethoven, Sonata Op. 2, No. 1, Minuet.

"Firm connection" means such a close interlocking of the motifs with one another and with their repetitions that the musical "shape" can no longer be regarded merely as the sum of the separate parts, but as an independent organic structure. This interlocking takes place firstly through an underpinning harmony or sequence of harmonies (e.g. I-V) which welds the motifs together (as in (a) above), or secondly through the overlapping of two motifs, so that the last note of one motif is also the first note of the following one (as in (b) ).

Larger sections of themes, e.g. antecedent and consequent (*Vordersatz und Nachsatz*), are linked together in a similar way; the consequent takes up the last note of the antecedent and this joint is also sealed harmonically. (In the following example from Beethoven's Op. 10, No. 1, this takes place through the Vth degree.)

Thus in the musical "shape" sections are created from the separate small parts, and are linked together firmly and irrevocably; they cannot be separated without destroying the parts. So the concept of a musical "shape" does not mean something put together ("composed"); it arises *a priori* as a whole, as a creative idea.

The whole collection of themes in a work, though apparently independent of one another, can be traced back to a single basic idea (as we shall show in detail with reference to Beethoven's Piano Sonata Op. 10, No. 1), whether or not one can recognise and demonstrate these relations in every case. This corresponds to the thesis that a work of art is a unity, the unity existing even where it cannot be exactly demonstrated.

If a basic idea of this kind takes on a musical shape, it thereby receives a quite definite and characteristic mould, a "musical character".

Now an idea can take on various shapes, and thus express various characters. The variation form is an example of this, and also shows (as, for instance, in Brahms' Paganini Variations), how development can go so far that no direct relationship between the theme and the variation can any longer be recognised.

In other words: the original shape which a basic idea assumes already contains the characteristics of the whole piece, both directly and indirectly. For, as we shall show at the end of this chapter, the whole thematic material of the piece is developed from this shape. We therefore call this the "basic shape" (*Grundgestalt*); it corresponds in its significance and functions to the "basic series" of twelve-note music.

In a piece of music we differentiate between main and subsidiary ideas. The main idea is the main theme developed out of the basic shape, or, where there are two or more main themes, the main thematic group. Opposed to the main idea—which, as we have said, contains all the preconditions and possibilities for the development of the piece—stands everything else derived from it; these are subsidiary ideas, either episodic, transitional or concluding. Their characteristics and formal functions depend on the constitution of the main idea, to which they are related in a "connected antithesis". Connected, because they are derived from it and from its basic shape; antithesis, because they introduce new shapes or characters which are contrasted with it.

An example of this can be seen in Beethoven's Sonata, Op. 10, No. 2:

Here the secondary theme shows an offshoot of the main idea. The characteristic features of the main theme retire into the background in the secondary theme, while others which were concealed in the main theme (bars 5 and 6) achieve their own importance and significance in the secondary theme.

Brahms, Piano Quartet in A minor:

These are examples of "developing variation"; out of unity comes diversity. Connections of this sort and their origins also have their parallel in twelve-note music.

The concept of the "connected antithesis" in music covers the most varied manifestations, and its importance for the creation of both tension and form is of the first order. Harmonically (in tonal music) it is found, for instance, between the main and the secondary themes. The latter is in the dominant key, the former in the related tonic key; both keys are different (antithesis) but related (connection). Again, both main and secondary themes stand in harmonic antithesis to the bridge-passage, which, as a modulating element, is in a state of motion, harmonically speaking. There is a parallel in the larger forms; the first part (exposition) and the third part (reprise) of a movement in sonata form centre on tonic-dominant (I-V), and are at rest harmonically; in contrast to this, the working-out section which lies between them is in motion harmonically. It moves through the various keys, and comes into contact with any of them except I and V; these latter are made conspicuous by their absence—presentation by exception, like saying "not dry" instead of "wet". The return to I-V in the reprise proves that in spite of all antithesis a harmonic coherence still exists, and that even the most far-reaching deviations have remained within the organic framework of the whole.

From the thematic and melodic point of view, the connected antithesis is demonstrated by the fact that out of one (basic) shape several different elements arise, which contrast both with it and with one another. These might first be contrasted with one another directly and in an unrelated manner, often with great dramatic tension (as in Mozart); and the idea of the piece might then consist in the surprising revelation later on of the connections between these contrasting thematic elements.

Similarly, but on a different level, we meet with the connected antithesis in the sphere of form, when tighter and looser formations together make up a theme (in ABA form, for instance) either simply in juxtaposition or linked together. Finally we find a connected antithesis in the fields of tone-colour and texture, when different sections contrast with one another, or are linked together, for instance by means of repetition. Incidentally, musical processes of this kind necessarily produce the most varied degrees and curves of tension.

We can see already that the *shape*, being the characteristic embodiment of a musical idea, is of supreme significance in the development of a musical work. Only that which has been "fixed" in the material in the form of a shape—whether it arises from a feeling, a mood or an extra-musical impression—goes beyond the cause which has released it, and only then does it become objective artistic expression in the purely musical sense. The cause remains implicit in it, but has been raised up and sublimated in the shape. In this complete and perfect transformation into music and in its "unravelling" lies one of the most essential difficulties in listening to and understanding music.

The invention of other subsidiary ideas, such as transitional and concluding ideas, from the basic shape of the main theme will be shown in the following pages. All subsidiary ideas have a purely functional purpose, working for the benefit of the main idea; in relation to the latter these may be digression, connection, preparation, interruption, transition, introduction, conclusion and so on. The form and structure of the themes vary according to their different purposes.

The three basic thematic forms are the sentence, the period, and the three-section (ABA) song-form. Each of these forms consists of the connection of a basic shape with its varied repetition. They differ from one another through the different ways in which the repetition of the basic shape takes place.

To make up the antecedent, the sentence form immediately repeats the basic shape on the same or another degree of the scale (harmonic variation), and then develops it further in the consequent.

Beethoven, Piano Sonata, Op. 2, No. 3, first movement:

32

On the other hand the period form immediately follows the basic shape with a further development of itself in the antecedent; the consequent repeats the whole of the antecedent. The antecedent and consequent are separated by a half-close on the dominant or some other division with a similar effect; Schoenberg compared the effect of this to a semicolon. So, in contrast to the sentence form, the period form is symmetrical; it is not so much the equal distance from the axis of symmetry that matters as the presence of this axis itself.

Beethoven, Piano Sonata, Op. 14, No. 1, Allegretto:

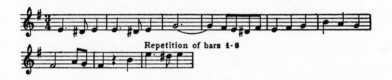

Repetition of bars 1-8

The symmetrical arrangement of the repetition, like the equality of the number of bars, is a strong means of increasing the comprehensibility of a theme. In opposition to the period form, the thematic sentence-form is more "modern", somewhat comparable with metrical prose. The formal structure is less constrained than in the period form; the lack of an axis of symmetry or central division allows the antecedent and consequent to be juxtaposed or antiposed in the most sharply contrasting manner, creating the maximum of tension. It is a dynamic form which is really "in motion", in contrast to the static, "resting" period form.

The three-section (ABA) thematic song form repeats the first section, which is solidly founded on the basic shape, after the second section has contained a "connected antithesis" to it. This latter may take the form of:

(a) A deviation from the basic shape,

(b) A new shape developed out of the first section,

(c) A development which breaks down or elaborates elements from the first section.

This is the suitable form for an idea which is so finite in its exposition that it demands no special working-out or extensive development; that which rests within itself, the song-like quality, is characteristic of this form.

The second section has the effect of a (protracted) caesura, like the axis of symmetry in the period form. Its structure is generally looser than that of the first and third sections which enclose it; these, which carry the weight of the musical content, contain correspondingly condensed formations in the form of phrases of two or more bars, while in contrast to this the middle section mostly produces short formations, often only one bar long; these—again in antithesis to the first and third sections—are loosely juxtaposed to one another.

The thematic form of the three-section song corresponds in the larger and more complex forms to the similarly-named form of the slow (Adagio) movement. If this case serves to confirm the thesis that all types of form-creation—the "thematic" as well as the higher ones—arise from the differing arrangement of the repetition of their sections, it is not difficult to show that this also applies to all the other classical forms—sonata form, scherzo, rondo. Indeed: *even if schemes of musical construction already exist in advance, they should not be consciously discovered until after they have been employed. To express oneself flexibly and clearly is an art which should be teachable.*[7]

It now remains to mention some other important means of construction in classical music and to show some parallels which are important for the technique of composition.

To avoid monotony, repetition demands variety. The latter arises from (a) the differentiation of the thematic characters mentioned above, or, in larger forms, of the different sections, e.g. between the exposition and the working-out in a sonata movement; (b) the differences in the formal construction; the structure, development and limitation; (c) in tonal music, the sequence of harmonies. These three belong together and are complementary to each other. The kind and amount of the differences in construction depend on the position and function of the themes. According to their structure we distinguish between tightly and loosely formed themes.

A characteristic of loose formation is the simple juxtaposition of different ideas. Examples of this can be found in Beethoven's Piano Sonata, Op. 2, No. 2, secondary theme in the first movement, bars 59–76; the group of secondary themes in Op. 2, No. 3, first movement, bars 27–61, and Op. 7, first movement, bars 24–56.

In tight forms the sections are firmly linked with one another. Thematic forms which remain in the same key, like main and secondary themes, are for that reason more tightly constructed than modulating sections like a bridge-passage, for instance, which is "in motion" harmonically and therefore has no power of definition. Where two sections meet each other, there is always a connection, of one of the following kinds:

(a) Harmonic. Example: Beethoven's Op. 10, No. 1, first movement, main theme, bars 4–5.

(b) Through a motivic relationship. Example: as (a), bars 9 and 10.

(c) The last note of one phrase is taken up by the following one. Example: as (a).

(d) Through the end of one phrase overlapping the beginning of the following one. Examples: Beethoven, Op. 13, first movement, Allegro, bars 3 and 5.

(e) Through a subsidiary part which brackets the two sections together. Examples: Beethoven, Op. 14, No. 2, Andante, bars 2–3; Op. 28, first movement, bars 5–10.

Compared with all other themes, a main theme shows relatively the tightest connection of its different sections. In addition, in classical music it is clearly marked off by an independent cadential section which is of no thematic importance; it merely serves to divide the main theme from the other themes. In the course of later development, in which the theme has to be flexible and mobile, it disappears, for the sake of a more fluid presentation of the ideas.

A secondary theme is more loosely formed than a main idea, but relatively more tightly than a transitional idea. It lacks the cadence which clearly marks off the main theme, and goes without any noticeable division into what follows.

If the main and secondary themes (or groups of themes) are the starting-point and the subject of development, the transitional and concluding (Codetta) ideas only take a very limited and local share in it by comparison. They are less a variation of a basic shape than a derivation or offshoot of it. They do not bring anything really new—in fact they should not; the task of the transition (bridge-passage) is to act as an intermediary, for instance between the main and secondary themes. For this purpose it must at one time be the one theme, at another the other, and therefore cannot have its own musical weight or content. The concluding idea must show the end of the presentation of the material, and must round it off. A new idea at this point would have the opposite effect, and would make the listener expect a continuation; but this would lead to lack of clarity in both content and form. Therefore as concluding ideas one mostly finds either a shape which is already known from what has gone before, or one which is seen in advance as already complete in itself, and does not make one expect any further development. It is repeated several times, varied either not at all or in an unimportant way, and at the same time it is reduced in length, by continually splitting off or leaving out characteristic parts of it. This means that the music is indeed still in motion, but it is as it were marking time. Together with this goes a reduction of its extent; for instance a four-bar concluding idea becomes a two-bar one, and this again is reduced to one bar. These all follow one on another, each of them being repeated without variation, loosely juxtaposed to one another, until ultimately only the final chord—also repeated several times—is left; the chest is nailed up. This type of Codetta or final section, which appears in the form described above in the classics (e.g. Haydn, Mozart), appears in a suitably altered form in contemporary music; for to-day we react more quickly to cadential elements, not only harmonic but also melodic and rhythmical ones, of the kind created by non-tonal music in the course of its development—under the compulsion of the disappearance of tonality and its power of creating a cadence.

The types of musical development and form-creation mentioned so far apply to *homophonic* classical music. They are based on the principle of repetition in conjunction with that of variation—or, more exactly, of variation o. the motif, and the transference of this in a suitable manner to larger musical forms. Development in polyphonic music (here we must not think of Bach, who represented the transition from the polyphonic to the homophonic style and unites both types of development in his music) indeed also depends on repetition, but in conjunction, not with motivic variation, but with motivic *working*.

This means that the motifs in a contrapuntal theme remain unaltered in their repetition not only in name, but also in the size of their intervals. A fugue subject (*dux*) must be answered within the so-called hexachord, in order to ensure this exact fixing of the intervals (in the *comes*). The same principle of the identical intervals applies to the twelve-note series, which, because of its perpetual repetition, also possesses as a whole the character of a motif. In homophonic music one part, the leading voice, carries the weight of the development; but in polyphonic music the development is carried out in two or more parts which are exactly equal to one another in importance. So quite different kinds and forms of development occur. The themes wander through the various parts and thereby experience the most varied musical fates. They are combined either with themselves or with other themes, sometimes loosely, sometimes tightly (e.g. the so-called stretto in the fugue), and this variation in the time of their successive appearances is increased by the possibility of exchanging the parts with one another; the upper part takes the place of the middle part at one time and of the bass part at another, and vice versa; these are then worked out according to the principles of double and multiple counterpoint. In addition to these possibilities of development—i.e. the varied thickening of the thematic texture right up to the stretto, by means of altering the distance in time between the various statements of the themes, and the variety achieved by exchanging the positions of the parts and their thematic content, which reveals new thematic combinations all the time—the following should also be mentioned: the use of augmentation and diminution of a theme by means of the exact doubling or halving of its note-values; the use of inversion (of the direction of the intervals), of cancrizans (or retrograde, the theme running backwards from the last note to the first) and of the inversion of the retrograde of a theme. This principle of construction, that of presenting a theme in its four possible forms of appearance, was frequently used by J. S. Bach, especially in his "Musical Offering" and "Art of Fugue"; it is also used in twelve-note composition.

It was necessary to set forth the principles of development and form in classical and polyphonic music, as formulated, taught, and used in his own music by Schoenberg, at least in their basic characteristics; for to know them and be able to handle them is a necessary precondition for composition with twelve notes, in which they are actively at work, and of which they constitute an integral part.

We shall end this chapter with an analysis and synthesis of Beethoven's Piano Sonata, Op. 10, No. 1, in C minor. This will show us that even in the music of the youthful Beethoven—who was composing in a relatively "unconscious" manner at that time—the creation of the themes of a whole work follows an idea of construction which is also of fundamental importance for Schoenberg's music in general, and for twelve-note music in particular; it is the idea that, in order to ensure the thematic unification of a work and thus the unity of its musical content, all the musical events in it are developed, directly or indirectly, out of one basic shape.

We shall begin with the thematic and formal analysis as generally practised. For the first movement, that in sonata form, we get the following picture (we shall start with the movement as a whole, and determine its division into larger sections; then from these sections we shall come to the smaller formal elements, the themes, phrases and motifs). The movement is clearly divided into three parts; the exposition lasts from bars 1–105, the working-out from bars 106–167, and the reprise from bars 168–284.

Exposition: Main theme   bars 1–22
         Transition  (a) liquidating the main theme, bars 23–31
                 (b) preparing for the secondary theme, bars 32–55
         Secondary theme, bars 56–76
         Liquidation of this and codetta, bars 77–105.

The 22-bar main theme is divided into three sections by two clearly marked caesuras, after bars 8 and 16. The third section (bars 17–22) is the cadential final section, which is not of importance thematically. By its very character it marks itself off from the second section just as clearly as this is marked off from the first. The first section again shows a clear division into two parts, and indeed a symmetrical one; bars 1–4 are immediately repeated, starting from the Vth degree (dominant), and, together with their repetition, form an eight-bar antecedent; the consequent (bars 9–16) shows a further development towards new shapes. Thus the whole theme is in a typical sentence form. The shape which occurs in the first four bars we shall call the basic shape.

So much for the analysis of the first movement. We will now continue it in another form, and in relation to the two other movements; and, starting from the basic musical shape, we shall show that this is the basis, not only of the main theme, but of the whole thematic material of the movement, and further of the whole work, and that not only are the *themes* derived from it, but also the subsidiary parts and figurations (see Tables I and II between pages 214 and 215).

The basic shape here consists of the firm connection of two elements which contrast sharply with each other, in dynamics, in musical character and in length; these are set in immediate juxtaposition to each other. The division of the bars is uneven:

3 + 1. The three-bars (a) are built in a complicated way. Here the first and last notes, C and E flat, are given special emphasis: the E flat through the rhythmical repetition with the up-beat, which gives it an accent, and the C through the compact chordal support of the tonic triad. Both notes are centres of gravity; they form a rising tenth (or minor third), an interval which does not appear again in the first movement, but acquires a motivic function in the Adagio movement which is of all the greater constructional importance. On the other hand the space of three bars bounded by these first and last notes is of immediate importance in the first movement. (Compare the rhythmical lay-out of the secondary theme.) The "up-beat" rhythm of the two crochet E flats is now taken up by the second motif (b) of the basic shape in bar 4, and connects the three-bar phrase with the one-bar phrase that follows it. Further, the three-bars contain, from the melodic point of view, a broken (tonic) triad; in conjunction with the characteristic dotted quaver rhythm and the repeated E flat at the end of the phrase, this forms that part of (a) which is important in the first movement.

These three-bars with their staccato ending are followed by a new motif (b), legato and piano in contrast to it; it consists of a falling second—minim C to crotchet B, with a crotchet C on the up-beat. Its firm connection with the preceding three bars is due both to the repetition of the note C which begins motif (a), supported by the same chord, and also to the immediate repetition of the "up-beat" rhythm E flat—E flat from the previous bar.

The joining together of the basic shape and its repetition to form the eight-bar antecedent is achieved (bars 4 to 5) through the harmonic bracket of the Vth degree, which seals the join together; melodically it occurs because the repetition begins with the same note B with which the basic shape ends. The further development of the first movement is dominated mainly by the motif (b).

Table I shows the direct and indirect connections which exist between the basic shape and the thematic material of the first movement which is developed from it, and also those between the themes themselves. It shows, in a clearer way than any words could do, the many possibilities of thematic development which can arise out of the four-bar basic shape, the unity of the shapes resulting from this, in spite of all the contrasts of the shapes among themselves, and the logic and homogeneity of the form and content. Schoenberg developed his method of composition with twelve notes on an analogous basis.

In the consequent of the main theme (bars 9–16) the content of the basic shape is considerably varied, and also condensed from four to two bars; motif (a) is reduced to an arpeggiated broken chord, and its final note G is also the beginning of a rhythmical variant ($b_1$) of the semitone motif (b), which then follows in an unvaried form. After the repetition of this new two-bar shape on the spot, without any developing variation of a harmonic, melodic or rhythmical kind (a halt in development which already prepares for the conclusion of the theme), motif (b), omitting the less important up-beat, forms a syncopated, descending sequence (bars 13–16). This kind of reduction has a "liquidating" effect; through the frequent repetition, without rhythmical or melodic alteration, of the dominating motif (b) in a form reduced to its essential falling second, it shows that no further development is to be expected and that the theme is approaching its end. It has already taken this path in bars 13–16.

The consequent introduces two new rhythmical motifs: ($b_1$) with dotted crotchet and quaver, and the syncopated crotchet figure. Both of these play a part in the later development.

In bars 14–16 the left hand takes up the rhythm of (b) and puts it against the syncopated sequence. But the combination of these two elements already forms the rhythmical core of bars 49–50— a similarity which is confirmed by the fact that both passages have a "liquidating" function.

The *transition* (or bridge-passage) is in two parts. The first (bars 23–30) liquidates the main theme; the second (bars 32–55) prepares for the secondary theme. The passage contains one new idea, a four-bar group (bars 33–36) formed from motif (b) by

41

the linking of two steps of a second downward—E flat—D flat—
(D flat—) C—circumscribed melodically by using the neigh-
bouring notes; this is combined with an enlargement of the
crotchet up-beat in the form of an upward leap of a sixth, G—
E flat. This, however, comes three times in motif (a) as a melodic
element, there as here in the form of an up-beat, and using exactly
the same notes; so this is a new, reduced variant of motif (a),
which now, together with the syncopated version of (b), forms
this transitional ideal. This is repeated several times, varied
only in harmony, and at the same time it brings the harmonic
transition, the modulation from C minor to the E flat of the
secondary theme. Shortly before the entrance of the latter, another
two-bar idea is introduced, on the dominant of E flat, in two-part
writing (bars 49–50). The upper part, with its up-beat of two
crotchets and its rhythmically shortened step of a second downwards, can quickly be recognised as a new variant of (b); further,
the rhythm is clearly derived from the four-bar transitional idea,
which it reduces to two bars, at the same time melodically loosen-
ing the suspension, which formerly was harmonically compact
and syncopated. At the same time, the accompanying lower part
goes in parallel, starting one bar (48) before the upper part; but
here the notes of the "falling-second" motif (b) are spread out
and placed on the first crotchet of each bar: A flat (49)—G (50)
—F (51)—E flat (52), concealed by the rhythmical regularity
of the crotchet movement on the weak beats.

Bars 53–55 carry the liquidation to its end; here the rhythm

of the upper part is dissolved by diminution, in regular quaver
movement. But this also prepares for the quaver movement in
the secondary theme (transition), and the melodic characteristic
of the falling second, C—B flat, A flat—G is levelled out note by
note by the quavers which surround it. Further compare bars
53–55 with bars 82ff, and with the Finale, bars 1–3.

*Secondary theme.* We have now considered the basic shape, in its content and form, its possibilities of development and its characteristics, in such detail that we shall not find it difficult to relate the origin of the secondary theme to it. The musical idea of the basic shape, that is to say, presentation by means of the opposition of two contrasting characters, each of which forms a motivic kernel, takes on a new shape in the secondary theme. It is similar in character to the transitional idea—so that it can appear after it, "prepared for and yet as a surprise"; but in contrast with the transitional idea it develops on a broad scale, pursuing its quite different formal function. It also makes a contrast in its harmonic disposition: remaining "at rest", it centres on I–V of E flat; whereas the transition is "in motion" from the harmonic point of view. Bars 56–57 show a new variant of the broken triad from motif (a), already prepared by the leap of a sixth in bar 33; on the other side this leans more closely towards the basic shape, up the ♩.♪♪ rhythm of the consequent (bars 9–10). It is connected as it occupies the same space of two bars as there, and also takes to motif (b) by the same note, E flat (58–59). There is a corresponding variant in bars 64–65, where, in place of the harmonic presentation of the tonic by means of a broken chord, its corresponding melodic presentation, the scale, appears; and at the same time, by giving up the characteristic leap of a sixth, it refers back to the development of the main theme, which in the corresponding place, the consequent (bars 9ff), limits itself to motif (b). Here, too, this reduction has a liquidating effect, and from bar 70 onwards continues it until the thematic shape is completely dissolved into a regular quaver movement (bars 82ff). We must note the artistic economy with which even such a subordinate element as the scalic figure on the weak beats (bars 48–49) is devoid of all arbitrariness—for instance, it appears worked into the quaver accompaniment of the secondary theme, and later contributes to the liquidation of this theme.

The derivation of the *concluding idea* (bars 95–98) from the basic shape—by means of bars 49–52, which also have a "concluding" effect—needs no explanation. But it is of importance that the quaver unison passage (bars 82–85) clearly refers back to bars 53–55, and shows a definite anticipation of the main theme of the Finale, both rhythmically and melodically (see Table II). Further, bars 79–82 are a slight variation of bars 71–74; but the latter arose out of the inversion of bars 33–36. In addition their connection is shown by the identity of the notes in their opening motifs (G—E flat and E flat—G) and also by their similar formal functions as transitional and liquidating sections respectively (Table II).

The *working-out section* finally introduces (bars 118–133), rather surprisingly, a new thematic shape; its strict formation underlines by contrast the "liquidating" character of the working-out. Its origin becomes clear if one compares its first four bars (118–122) with the transitional idea (bars 33–36), and bars 122–125 with the first four bars (56–59) of the secondary theme. So this new combination reveals the affinity between the transitional and secondary themes, and shows new and direct connections in the form of a new thematic shape. Further, the appearance, surprising in itself, of such a long self-contained theme in a section so loosely constructed, and with such a "dissolving" effect as a working-out section, is sensed by one's feeling for form as a counterweight to the remarkably varied lay-out of the exposition. A purely "dissolving" treatment of the working-out could not create a formal counterweight to such an exposition.

Finally, bars 159–162 (with up-beat) bring a new shape, which is developed from bars 13–16, using the same notes and intervals —a model example of "developing variation".

It is really remarkable when we look at the other movements of the sonata from the same point of view. For these also reveal that their themes are derived from the basic shape of the first movement, which can therefore be regarded as the basic shape of the whole sonata (see Table II).

To repeat: it is completely unimportant whether one regards this creative process, wholly or partially, as conscious or unconscious. The only essential and decisive thing is that these connections exist. This demonstration of the truth that a work of art is a unity also remains valid if in one case or another it is not so completely conclusive or is not conclusive at all; the presence of something and the perception of it are two different things.

Just as the thematic material of a tonal work is derived from the basic shape, similarly in twelve-note music it arises out of the basic set (series).

## CHAPTER IV

# THE THEORETICAL AND MUSICAL BASES OF SCHOENBERG'S COMPOSITION WITH TWELVE NOTES

*The emancipation of the dissonance—The "Magic Square"—The "Musical Space"—Synthesis of homophonic and polyphonic development in Schoenberg's music*

BEFORE going on to a practical explanation of the method of composition with twelve notes, we must first familiarise ourselves with three concepts which were stated and formulated by Schoenberg, as well as with the difference between the homophonic and polyphonic methods of composition.

Parallel to, and in reciprocal relation with the development which led during the last hundred years to the weakening and finally to the suspension of tonality, a process was completed which, as a result of the musical development of this epoch, brought with it a radical alteration of the concepts of consonance and dissonance.

In his *Harmonielehre*, which appeared in 1911, Schoenberg already maintained that dissonant notes were really more distant consonances, i.e. overtones which are more distant from the fundamental note. The relativeness of the concept of dissonance is shown by the fact that the same interval may be felt by one hearer as consonant and by another as dissonant. This all goes to show how right was Schoenberg's idea of bringing all relations between notes together in the unified concept of the nearer and more distant consonances—this also anticipates all further possibilities in the development of the human ear. The development of music as well as that of our musical ear confirm this view. The continuous employment of more and more acute dissonances, at first prepared and resolved by means of consonances, then appearing quite freely as the ear was prepared to accept them with increasing confidence, made these more and more easily comprehensible; more and more they lost the effect of interrupting the musical sense. This can be traced from the early days when the third still counted as not a perfect consonant, to the "emancipated" appearance of the diminished seventh in classical music—that is to say, a diminished seventh which was freed from the need to be prepared and resolved by a consonance—and, further, to the free use of augmented triads and even more acutely dissonant intervals and chords in the second half of the nineteenth century. The ear accepted these musical phenomena in the works of our great masters, and in time also understood "very remote" consonances direct, without needing to explain them by relating them to a key-note and demonstrating their tonal relationships every time they appeared.

It is clear that this progressive *Emancipation of the Dissonance* accelerated the weakening of tonality at the same time; as the dissonance appeared unprepared and disappeared equally abruptly, it made the demonstration of its tonal origin more and more superfluous, and the dominance of the key-note more and more questionable. From this development Schoenberg drew the conclusion, both in his own music and in theoretical perception, that *what distinguishes dissonances from consonances is not a greater or lesser degree of beauty, but a greater or lesser degree of comprehensibility.* And: *The term emancipation of the dissonance refers to its comprehensibility, which is considered equivalent to the consonance's comprehensibility. A style based on this premise treats dissonances like consonances and renounces a tonal centre.*[2]

*The "Musical Space"* We have already spoken, in connection with the concept of form, of the affinities within the actual material of music. Each note has affinity with a note which lies a fifth below it. The lower notes are the homeland, as it were, of the higher. The mental ear hears a note and its harmonic series at the same time; how else could we have discovered the octave? It is only because we unconsciously felt it as belonging to this one note that we accepted it as comprehensible when it in fact appeared. In the same way we discovered the major triad, and so on. In his *Harmonielehre* Schoenberg already pointed out that a note can be understood in both its vertical and its horizontal implications: that is to say, its overtones can be presented simultaneously in a chord or arranged one after another in a scale. The simultaneity of the notes of a chord can be changed into consecutiveness: *Melody is the unconscious recognition, obtained from immediate intuition, of the unity of time and space in relation to music.*[6]

In rhythm we find the imitation of sounds of different pitch translated into the dimension of time. The octave = two-part rhythm; the fifth (fundamental note with the octave and fifth as overtones) = three-part rhythm.

Schoenberg recognised that this correspondence between simultaneity and consecutiveness, which allowed him to present a note in two different ways, was an important unifying principle of musical composition because of its effect on the musical organism. He compared it to the "Magic Square", in which the same letters form the same words and the same meaning, both horizontally and vertically.

In tonal music this relation was maintained through tonality. Here the melodic elements—broken chords and scale fragments— found harmonic elements which fully corresponded to them, for both were derived from the same source—tonality. The effect of this was a close co-ordination of the melodic and the harmonic phenomena.

Tonality's function of ensuring this connection had to be taken over by the twelve-note series in twelve-note music. For both of these, tonality and note-series, were indeed integral constituents of the first creative conception of a work; thus they arose organically from this conception, and at the same time brought the raw material of music, the notes, into an order which fulfilled a musical purpose and obeyed its laws.

This was a fundamental perception for the method of composition with twelve notes. It was combined with an extraordinarily intuitive comparison on Schoenberg's part concerning the process of composition, which brings time and space into a relation similar to the definition of melody quoted above; *Music is an art which takes place in time. But the way in which a work presents itself to a composer (= vision = intuition = inner hearing) is independent of this; time is regarded as space. In writing the work down, space is transformed into time. For the hearer this takes place the other way round; it is only after the work has run its course in time that he can see it as a whole—its idea, its form and its content.*[6]

From here it was only a step, though a very important one in its consequences for the technique of composition, to the establishment of the concept of "Musical Space":

*Music is not merely another kind of amusement, but a musical poet's, a musical thinker's representation of musical ideas; these musical ideas must correspond to the laws of human logic; they are a part of what man can perceive, reason and express. Proceeding from these assumptions, I arrived at the following conclusions:*

*THE TWO-OR-MORE-DIMENSIONAL SPACE IN WHICH MUSICAL IDEAS ARE PRESENTED IS A UNIT. Though the elements of these ideas appear separate and independent to the eye and the ear, they reveal their true meaning only through their co-operation, even as no single word alone can express a thought without relation to other words. All that happens at any point of this musical space has more than a local effect. It functions not only in its own plane, but also in all other directions and planes, and is not without influence even at remote points.*[2]

Schoenberg gives as an example the effect of progressive rhythmical subdivision, which rests on the "tendency of the shortest notes" to multiply themselves, and which can be observed in every classical composition. An example of another kind is given by Brahms' Variations on a theme of Handel. The theme and the first four variations are in the key of B flat major. At the beginning of the first bar of the second variation the note D flat appears in a middle part, at first in a quite inconspicuous and transitional manner, in the form of a chromatic passing note, D—D flat—C. It is repeated on the third crotchet of the same bar, but now in a slightly more conspicuous manner, being in the upper part;

but it still only has a subordinate function, as a C sharp having the effect of a leading note on to the D of the melody. Then it appears at the end of the second bar as a melodic passing note, C—C sharp—D, and from now on becomes more and more prominent, but still without endangering B flat major; not even when, later on, the note which has been introduced in the way we have seen appears for the first time as a D flat within the scale in the upper part of bar 9 (C—B—C—D flat—C—B flat). There, too, it still belongs harmonically to B flat major, to the region of its subdominant minor, as the continuation shows. However, in the same place in the third variation, which still remains in the fundamental key, we find the note D flat, this time not melodically, but in the compacter harmonic group B flat—D flat—F. In the following bar it differs from the second variation by going another step further in this direction; the G flat (—B flat—E flat) in the bass lends emphasis to the minor character of the tonic B flat—D flat—F, but still without putting B flat major in question. In the next variation this development, which is tending towards B flat minor, now also includes the immediate surroundings, bars 9 and 10. The time is now ripe for a decision, and the fifth variation brings it, with the change of key to B flat minor which has been prepared for so long before. The unthematic note D flat, which at first appeared so inconspicuously, and then remained of only local importance, has gradually and consistently pushed itself through in more and more remote places, and in different planes (the harmonic and the melodic) of the musical space of this set of variations.

This example clearly shows the far-reaching theoretical and practical perspectives which Schoenberg's definition of the "Musical Space" opens up. If such a small element as a single note is capable of such a far-reaching effect within the musical space, such effects will be correspondingly greater where motifs or themes are concerned.

In parenthesis: the concept of the emancipation of the dissonance also acquires a heightened meaning from the aspect of the "musical space". Emancipation means the guaranteeing of equal rights and equal entitlements. The moment one note claims rights equal to those of all the other notes, it no longer recognises the domination of any other note. It emancipates itself from the key-note, which had dominated it up till then; the existence of the key-note was based essentially on the mere fact that it divided the notes into two classes—those that were nearer to it and those that were further from it, i.e. consonances and dissonances. But in musical space there are only greater or lesser distances between the notes in relation to one another, not merely the distances outwards from a tonal centre, and the greater or lesser comprehensibility of their connections with one another corresponds to these distances. This permits a unified perception of all thinkable connections of notes (i.e. combinations of notes sounded together); they only differ from one another in a *gradated* manner, and thus make it superfluous to divide them into separate classes, as consonances or dissonances. There are only consonances now; dissonances are merely more remote consonances. The whole matter is relative, and it is left entirely to the musical education of our ears to reduce these distances and bring more distant combinations of notes "nearer". What we have said confirms the fact that this process (up to the thirteenth century, for instance, the third was considered to be an imperfect consonance) has continued to progress up to the present day and is by no means complete yet.

From this view of music in space, and from the perception that a musical idea is not merely a melody, nor merely a harmony or a rhythm, but a combination of these three elements, came the further conclusion that: *The elements of a musical idea are partly incorporated in the horizontal plane as successive sounds, and partly in the vertical plane as simultaneous sounds. The mutual relation of tones regulates the succession of intervals as well as their association into harmonies; the rhythm regulates the succession of tones as well as the succession of harmonies and organises phrasing.*[2]

The perception of these facts had decisive results for composition with twelve notes; for it made it possible to use a basic series of twelve notes, as a whole or in parts, in either dimension

—that is to say, allowing its notes or note-sequences to appear both vertically in a chord and horizontally in a melodic formation; the choice of each being determined by the demands of the composition.

All our theoretical and analytical examinations and conclusions so far have been essentially concerned with homophonic music. But as composition with twelve notes, like tonal composition, also includes contrapuntal writing in several parts—either pure, or mixed or synthesised with the homophonic style—we must now consider some more of the characteristic features of polyphonic music and their effects on composition in order to complete the picture. There is all the more reason for this, as Schoenberg himself used both homophonic and contrapuntal methods to a very great extent even in his early tonal works. This was naturally also reflected in his twelve-note compositions, in a synthesis which by then had become completely matured; thus many of the features of the technique of composition according to his method are of contrapuntal origin—which does not, however, prevent their being also used in a purely homophonic manner.

The homophonic music, which came after the polyphonic age, followed an entirely new path from the point of view of musical presentation and development. Externally it appeared to have undertaken the task of expressing itself in a clearly comprehensible manner, after the complications of the polyphonic epoch, and of ensuring the wide understanding of a musical idea. In order to be able to carry out this task, it let all the other parts retire into the background for the benefit of one single part, the main part, which alone carried the musical idea and its development. The broad structure which a theme made of broken chords (still to be found in Wagner) possessed through its relation to one harmony, permitted development to go further in a different direction; the principle of variation went beyond the motif and included the basic shape of the work, from which it caused new elements to grow.

This led, in the period from Bach to Brahms, to the development of new forms of an unheard-of richness, which the poly-phonically constructed music of the twentieth century also used. Harmony no longer arises more or less without any obligation, through the movement of the parts, but is a fundamental phenomenon, and is treated as such.

On the other hand, contrapuntal music, in its development up to Bach, allows the individual parts comparatively little room for independent development. Instead of variation of the motif, which acts as the motive power in classical homophonic music, in polyphonic music we find "motivic working". This means that the motif itself remains unaltered, and the musical develop-ment chiefly resides in (1) the variation in the number of the parts, and above all the varying of the disposition of the parts through the use of double and multiple counterpoint, (2) the variation in time of the entries of the parts (or of the motivic or thematic figures), and (3) the combination of both of these possibilities of variation.

A contrapuntal idea is invented without reference to harmony. Its structure is different from that of a homophonic theme; broken chords in a theme are practically impossible,* and, above all, the way it is "worked" is such that it cannot be made up out of chords. A contrapuntal theme is difficult to grasp from the harmonic point of view; it is based on many harmonies or else none at all, and the harmonies which arise out of the movement of the parts are not "obligatory"—their succession has no func-tional importance. It is therefore short—in contrast to a homo-phonic theme—and this is necessary for its varied wanderings through the different parts, so as to give it the desired mobility and versatility.

Contrapuntal music too has a kind of "basic shape" in the form of a connection together of several short motifs; but, in contrast to homophonic music, no new shapes are evolved from it. One can say that the subject and counter-subject of a fugue correspond to the antecedent and consequent of a homophonic theme. In the

---

* Bach, as a transitional phenomenon, combines homophonic and polyphonic elements in his music.

latter both sections of the theme are heard in succession and firmly joined together (by means of harmony), while in contrapuntal music they appear at the same time and are connected by this simultaneity. The connection here is a more elastic one, and the feeling of belonging together is not so strong; the subject and counter-subject are two relatively independent parts of a whole, easier to release from their links, and capable of changing places with each other or being separated, corresponding to the methods of counterpoint; this makes them all the more consistent and invariable in themselves. This principle of "motivic working" which forbids all variation of the intervals can be seen most clearly in the tonal answer to a fugal theme; according to the rules of strict counterpoint this has to follow in the so-called hexachord, which ensures the exact, unaltered repetition (*comes*) of the subject (*dux*), not only in name, but in the actual size of its intervals.

The extraordinarily strong prohibitions contained in this and other laws of contrapuntal writing go far beyond what composition with twelve notes demands in this respect.

## CHAPTER V

SERIAL COMPOSITION IN SCHOENBERG'S OP. 23 AND 24 AS THE
PRECURSOR OF COMPOSITION WITH TWELVE NOTES

*The basic conception* (Grundgestalt) *as a musical law
—The fields of force in music and their changes—
The melodic motif—The basic shape as containing
the musical thought—The note-series as a melodic
extract of the basic shape—The Five Piano Pieces,
Op. 23, and the Serenade, Op. 24*

IN THE development which led to the method of composition
with twelve notes, two works of Schoenberg hold a key position
from several points of view: the Five Piano Pieces, Op. 23, and
the Serenade, Op. 24 (both published by Hansen, Copenhagen).
They come between the Four Songs with Orchestra, Op. 22, which
were still written in the free non-tonal style, and the first purely
twelve-note composition, the Suite for Piano, Op. 25, and they
represent a transition from one method of composition to the
other. These circumstances, as well as the fact that they contain
twelve-note movements (the last of the Five Piano Pieces and the
fourth movement of the Serenade) together with others in the
free non-tonal style, show Schoenberg's completely undoctrinaire
attitude; to him it only mattered that music was good and had
something to say, but it never mattered on what principle it was
constructed. Some movements of the Suite were written before
the twelve-note parts of Op. 23 and 24, while these latter works
were completed during the two years following. The "equal
birth" of these musical organisms of different kinds, as well as
the fact that Schoenberg's work on them overlapped in time,
makes it clear that the birth and growth of twelve-note composition was a natural one, and that its development was com-

pletely evolutionary, nurtured and directed by the musical imagination. *

The works mentioned above show this development as it were *in statu nascendi*, and so allow us to perceive with special clarity the idea which afterwards found its practical expression in Schoenberg's method. Apart from the intellectual stimulus which one obtains from watching the birth of a new compositional process, we wish to study these works—and particularly the non-twelve-note parts of them—for an eminently practical reason: because this phase of Schoenberg's development shows such manifold possibilities which could be followed up individually, and these possibilities give so much scope in their choice, use and combination, that from this point other paths besides Schoenberg's method of composition also become visible. One of these was entered on occasions by Schoenberg himself in the two last decades of his life, in compositions which combine the elements of the major-minor tonality and the modal scales with elements of serial composition.

To follow step by step the realisation of the idea of twelve-note composition in practice has the advantage that one is able to acquire an exact knowledge of the forces that are active in it, and of their close organic connections with each other and with tradition, thereby immediately obtaining a clue towards handling it for the practice of composition. What was its point of departure? From what grouping of the musical forces did this idea arise, and for what purpose?

In tonal music two fields of force are at work. One of them is so to speak of dual power, for its energies arise from the combination of the melodic and the rhythmical elements and create motivic and thematic (i.e. melodic) shapes. The other field of force is that of tonality, which is preponderantly harmonic. Each of these fields of force produces energies out of itself; the latter by the perpetual variation of harmonic formations and sequences of chords with differing degrees of tension, the former through changing combinations and variations of the melodic (i.e. the intervals) and the rhythmical elements.

The very varied interplay of both fields of force acts as the motive power of the course of the music. The way in which this interplay takes place represents the musical idea which is the basis of the piece and is a product of the creative imagination. It is formed by the musical inspiration and comes from it; we therefore call it the *basic shape* (*Grundgestalt*).* Out of this the composer evolves the work following his original conception, which allows him first to see it as a whole in his mind and to form and shape it accordingly. In this complex sense the idea too is an "inspiration", whether consciously or unconsciously.

The basic shape contains in its disposition both the fields of force, between which the work "plays"—the basic tonality and the basic motivic content. Everything else arises from these, so that one can truly say: the original conception (= the basic shape) contains the *law* of the whole work and is the first precise formulation of it. As we shall see, this applies both to tonal and to twelve-note music. In tonal music both the fields of force are held together by the co-ordination of the melodic and the harmonic elements; for in tonal music the motif (or theme or melody) is derived from the key. Here it does not matter whether one gives priority to the harmonic or to the melodic element; the only thing that matters is that the two elements correspond with each other, in both the vertical and horizontal dimensions† and in their complementary interplay.

Furthermore, the energies emanating from the fields of force mentioned above naturally control every individual note, and define it in a twofold manner, as a melody note or as a harmony

---

* In his *Betrachtungen und Erinnerungen* (Atlantis Verlag, Zurich and Freiburg) Richard Strauss writes in the essay "On Melodic Invention": "To give my own experience in creative work: a motif or a two- to four-bar melodic phrase occurs to me immediately. I write it down and at once extend it into a phrase of eight, sixteen or thirty-two bars; naturally this does not remain unaltered, but after leaving it alone for a longer or shorter time it is gradually worked out into its final form. In the course of this it has to endure the strictest and most sophisticated self-criticism." The first sentence of this quotation completely and surprisingly bears out our supposition that the basic shape already represents the whole conception of a work and is the starting-point of the musical "working-out".

† See Schoenberg, *Models for Beginners in Composition*, Schirmer, New York.

note (these two functions may be simultaneous or alternative); the latter definition is based on the relationship of the individual note to the key-note, the former definition results from the fact that it is part of the motivic and thematic (melodic) material, and from its function in it. Both are integrating principles, which create "order and unity" in the musical organism. Both are dependent on each other, due to the co-ordination of the melodic and harmonic elements, which is an essential condition of the unity of a piece of music.

As we showed with examples in one of the previous chapters, when thematic and melodic development, with its increasing tendency towards dodecaphony, allowed the connection with the field of force which was centred on tonality to become looser and looser, until the latter finally was dissolved, the individual note was compelled to lose one of its two means of definition, that based on its key. But the importance of the remaining motivic-thematic definition increased in equal measure, and it was now the only definition, in free non-tonal music, on which the note depended; it was now the only means of preserving the musical coherence, order and unity of the whole organism. The increased strain put upon it led to the elements which now remained—that is to say the rhythmical and melodic elements—being intensified, concentrated and more greatly differentiated in themselves. So one of the consequences of this development was the increasing use of contrapuntal writing and polyphony, starting simultaneously with many composers at the beginning of the twentieth century; this does not provide musical coherence by means of the constructional power of chord-sequences, but through the intertwining of several parts, that is to say by melodic means. After the abandonment of tonality, the harmonic element could no longer be used as a means of definition which could create form or coherence.

The first of Schoenberg's Three Piano Pieces, Op. 11, already shows the alteration of the musical structure indicated above, in its interlacing of motifs which produce and reveal relationships, and in its extremely close intertwining of the motivic (thematic) material. It begins with a theme of eleven (3 + 5 + 3) bars, in three sections:

This is clearly divided into three parts. All the musical ideas in the piece can be traced back to the three-bar basic shape (bars 1–3). But it should be noticed that the harmonic structure, too, in spite of the absence of any tonal organisation, is in no way arbitrary: it is based on the first two chords in bars 2 and 3, i.e. on the intervals in them. In contrast to the three-bar first and third sections, which are homophonic, the five-bar middle section has a four-part shape, which is repeated twice and harmonically is relatively "at rest" (pedal point on G sharp). Although each of the four parts is repeated exactly from the melodic point of view, a multiple variation of the four-part shape is obtained, as the four parts appear at constantly varying moments in time in relation to one another, and this causes new arrangements of the elements each time, which are also different harmonically—a typically contrapuntal method of procedure.

The later Six Little Piano Pieces, Op. 19, present another aspect. These are essentially pieces of an aphoristic brevity, which makes it possible to comprehend and survey the whole of each one, both in form and content, in one breath, as it were; thus no particular formal methods are necessary. In pieces of six to seventeen bars' length no development is possible; this would naturally have required a more differentiated formation. Thus here the form is limited to the shape of the aphoristic thought.

The real problem first arose in the case of works of greater length, especially when they could not prop themselves up by being combined with words or follow the form and disposition of a poem. It was clear to Schoenberg that in place of the field of force which was defined by tonality, a new one must be found which stood in a similar relationship to the motivic and thematic field of force as the harmonic one had done previously; it must be capable of a similar interplay with it for the purpose of creating form and content; it must also give some kind of order to the material structure of the notes which has to be meaningful and of compositional value. To put it in a few words: in place of the lost definition with reference to the key, and in addition to the motivic and thematic definition which still remained, the individual note must find a new means of definition. But if (as could not be doubted) the *law* of a piece of music is contained in its central conception (or idea), the new field of force and the new means of definition, with corresponding formative powers, could only come from this conception. Schoenberg perceived and found these first of all in the melodic "fixing" (or arrangement) of the notes made by the "conception" embodied in a musical shape. The idea and development of this last phase before twelve-note composition can be demonstrated in this way: every individual note in an original conception, in the basic shape, has a definite interval-relationship to the notes which precede and follow it. This relationship is only determined by the melodic logic of the basic musical conception, as tonality's powers of definition have disappeared. The sequence of notes and intervals fixed by means of the basic conception thus gives, *a priori*, an organisation with a musical purpose, that is to say, a melodic definition which (as we saw in Beethoven's Op. 10, No. 1) was already present in tonal music, even if not in such a dominant manner. This sequence of notes is, as it were, the pure melodic extract from the basic musical conception, and, being an integral part of the latter, is just as responsible for the whole piece as is the basic conception itself. In order that a melodic field of force which permeates the whole musical organism may arise from this sequence of notes, and combine itself with the motivic and thematic field of force—as the harmonic field of force or tonality does in tonal music—this field of force must control the melodic structure of the piece. This takes place when this sequence of notes, which is legitimised by the original conception, takes on the function of a purely melodic motif—by means of continuous repetition of the note-sequence, irrespective of its rhythmical treatment or of its simultaneous alterations from the motivic and thematic point of view.

In parenthesis: the formal function of a motif—i.e., its function of giving coherence—rests in its frequent repetition; this is how it is recognisable. Thus the continual repetition of a note-series derived from the basic conception gives this series the function of a motif.

To sum up: with the decay of the harmonic field of force, the dual power—to keep the same metaphor—of the motivic and thematic field of force was split into two. Its melodic element was freed, and developed its own field of force, which took the place of the harmonic field. (Meanwhile, as we shall see later, the rhythmical field also developed on its own and acquired a more independent importance outside the melodic sphere.) The melodic "infiltration" which arose from the perpetual repetition of the note-series had the same effect as that of tonal harmony; it gave a musically purposive definition of the sound-material, it ensured the co-ordination between the harmonic and the melodic components of a piece, and also the unity of the musical organism, which was considerably strengthened by this co-ordination. All this created the basic conditions for the logical construction of forms which could contain musical development on a larger scale; this was finally made possible through composition with twelve notes.

But this stage had not yet been reached. In the first four of the Five Piano Pieces, Op. 23, and in the variation movement of the

Serenade, Op. 24, Schoenberg does not yet use all the twelve notes of the well-tempered system in the way described above, for the basic thematic shapes here produce note-series of less than twelve different notes, of which some are repeated in certain circumstances. But the series are mostly used in the manner of the later twelve-note series, and are already handled with a compositional freedom within this law which does not allow the presence of the law itself to be consciously felt.

The following eleven-bar theme of the variation movement of the Serenade is a unison one; the clarinet plays it without any accompaniment.* It contains only eleven different notes, of which three are repeated; the note B is missing. These fourteen notes are the melodic foundation of the antecedent (bars 1–6):

The consequent (bars 7–11), following classical procedure, is a slightly varied repetition of the antecedent in its content, i.e. its shapes; but its melodic course follows the retrograde form of the fourteen-note basic series. The last note, F, of the original is also the first note of the retrograde form.

What is the musical purpose of this retrograde melodic form in the second half of the theme? The answer is as surprising as it is convincing: this is a "mirroring" of the *melodic* sequence of the antecedent, exactly as in a corresponding tonal theme the *harmonic* sequence I–V in the antecedent is "mirrored" in the V–I of the consequent; the melodic law takes the place of the harmonic. The formal effect of the symmetrical division is the same. Further, the theme begins and ends with the same note,

---

In the musical examples, including the Tables, all transposing instruments are written as they sound.

B flat. This corresponds to a rule of contrapuntal writing, according to which the part which begins a piece must begin and end on the key-note. Also, the last note of the antecedent and the first note of the consequent is the same note, F. This stands to B flat in the relation of a fifth (I–V); as we shall see later (p. 95), this is no accident.

We can already see from this example, taken from a "precursor" of twelve-note composition, that the use of mirror forms (inversion, retrograde and retrograde inversion), which in any case were a matter of course in the music of the fifteenth and sixteenth centuries, is nothing accidental or arbitrary (compare the Beethoven theme, p. 12). It acquires even more point from the conception of the Musical Space, the multi-dimensional quality of which particularly corresponds to contrapuntal music. This "spatial" perception of a musical idea allows it forms of appearance which change in perspective; but in spite of all differences they remain the same because of their unchanging identical structure. This applies to the handling of the series in respect of its continual repetition as a melodic motif; it can be repeated in the original form or in one of the three mirror forms. Thus the law concerning the series—irrespective of whether it is a series of twelve, or fewer, or more notes—shows that it can be "followed strictly and yet handled freely".

Schoenberg made the identity of the four forms of a series clear by this comparison: an object, for example a hat or a bottle, when viewed from different sides presents a different appearance each time, although it still remains the same hat or bottle. What applies to material things is possible in a far higher degree with imagination and the power of spiritual perception: . . . *a musical creator's mind can operate subconsciously with a row of tones, regardless of their direction, regardless of the way in which a mirror might show the mutual relations, which remain a given quantity.*[2]

In addition to the formal effects produced by the retrograde form of a series (which have already been mentioned, and which apply correspondingly to its inversion and retrograde inversion), further advantages may be gained from the melodic variation caused by the three mirror forms. This can be shown by a comparison of the corresponding passages in the antecedent and consequent, e.g. bars 1–3 with 6–8, or bar 5 with bar 9. This type of variation, which sometimes goes very far, is a natural counterbalance to the continuous repetition of the series and the danger of monotony which this brings. (In the next chapter we shall deal in detail with other means, of several different kinds, of avoiding this danger.) But the rhythm ensures that thematic formations which are varied in this way still remain recognisable to the listener as what they are. The part played by rhythm in building musical shapes becomes greater in twelve-note music (and in serial music generally), through the marked character and individual contours of the rhythmical motifs, in proportion to the importance of the part played in the piece by the shape itself. One can say quite simply "by their rhythm shall ye know them"—not only the musical shapes themselves, but also their functions and their position in the whole musical organisation of the piece. The straightforwardness or the subtlety of the rhythmical structure is not merely a general characteristic of the individual style of the composer; but the contrast and variation between straightforward and subtle rhythm often indicates the formal function of the shape. For example, a transitional idea is generally more straightforward and less complicated rhythmically, while a main idea is richer and has more subtle ramifications. Rhythm has a double function: it can create musical shapes—compare, for instance, the clarinet part in bar 40, p. 68, with the viola part in bar 35, p. 67; and it can build forms, for instance as a motivic "main rhythm" in the last movement of Alban Berg's Chamber Concerto; or as a kind of rhythmical "pedal-point" it makes larger sections of a form cohere, or helps to create them, as in the first movement of Schoenberg's third String Quartet. This chapter on rhythm has yet to be written, and Schoenberg's twelve-note works provide a wealth of material for the purpose; for they show quite new relations between melody and rhythm, as the two elements which create musical shapes.

But this makes something else clear, namely the dominating

rôle which the musical shape itself, as the characteristic means of expressing a musical idea, acquires in Schoenberg's music. The musical shape is the primary consequence of an idea, and is its presentation in actual sound. The idea must assume a shape in order to communicate itself to us in and through this shape, and in order to be recognised and understood. The conception of the musical shape is an important means of appreciating Schoenbergian music. The richer and more complicated the development of the music, the clearer and more flexible must be the form wherein this development is demonstrated—that is to say, the musical shape.

Thus the five variations in the Serenade show important variants of the basic shape of the theme shown above. For this purpose they use, in a closely intertwined manner, the classical variation technique of Beethoven and Brahms, carried further forward by Schoenberg, and also the fourteen-note series and its three mirror forms. From these latter and their transpositions on to other notes—this is another possibility allowed by the serial technique—there arise

(a) chords:

(b) subsidiary parts:

(c) accompanying figures:

Either one part can follow one form of the series, as in (b) and (c), or the musical conception may require a series to be split up and divided between two parts, in the form of chords, as in (a), or in a linear manner as in (d):

(d)

This depends on the demands of the musical conception in one place or another; for it is always this which creates the note, or notes. (The examples are from the third movement of Schoenberg's Serenade, Op. 24.)

Wherever one opens the score of the Serenade, the music leaps to one's eye; one word leads to another, as it were. Let us take any bar of the variation movement—for instance the beginning of the third variation, which begins in the clarinet on the up-beat before bar 35 (d). The main part, a one-bar phrase in the clarinet, is intertwined with its own imitative inversion in the bass clarinet, making a two-bar phrase. This, in combination with the characteristic contrasting semiquaver movement in the other instruments, forms a new shape, and its sequence of notes is not derived from the basic series. Where does it come from?

Let us look at the bass part (in the 'cello) of the group of chords in (a), bars 27–28. There we find the same sequence of notes as still unformed raw material; it is part of the sequence of chords formed from the retrograde inversion. In (d) it is fully formed and has become the main part, combined with the accompaniment to form a characteristic shape. It represents notes 1, 2, 6, 7 and 8 of the basic series, while the mandoline plays notes 3, 4, 5 and 9 as an accompaniment. (Through its musical subdivision the fourteen-note series is split into a nine-note and a five-note section. This subdivision of the series and the use of these sections as independent small series will be found again in twelve-note music too.)

The "thickening" of the sound which is necessary here brings in the violin and viola with the help of the inversion of the basic series. From the five semiquavers of the accompanying viola part (see also the violin part in bars 27–28), the main part in the clarinet in bar 40 is later developed.

The imitative inversion of this in the 'cello (bar 41) is then combined with the main part of bar 35 (p. 67) to form a four-bar melody, which ends this variation. This again leads to something new: the subsidiary part in the clarinet, which "comments" on this four-bar phrase, leads through into the fourth variation, which begins in the following bar. This is an entirely new melody, the beginning of which is clearly a variation of the beginning of the

main theme (bars 1–2); meanwhile the main phrase (bars 35 ff.) of the previous variation now retires to become an accompanying subsidiary part. At this point we remember having already heard this melodic sequence before the second variation, as a cadential clarinet passage which ends the first variation; here it again clearly quotes the characteristic beginning of the theme (bars 1–2), but in retrograde inversion.

Before concluding these analytical examples from the Serenade —the analysis of the whole work would fill a book—there is still something to be said about Example (a). It shows that a series— in this case the retrograde inversion—can form chords, and in what way it does so. This depends on the fact that the vertical and horizontal components of music are co-ordinated, whether it be tonal music or not. As applied to twelve-note composition, it means that the same notes (or the intervals formed by them) which, in conjunction with the rhythm, shape the horizontal course of a musical idea, can also be combined in the vertical dimension into one or more chords; that is to say, without rhythm, but containing the same intervals. The co-ordination which is attained in this way between the two dimensions of music—a co-ordination which has its prototype in the canon and stretto of contrapuntal music—and the homogeneity and unification of the music which is arrived at by this means are plain to see. The melodic extract of a musical idea can also assume a harmonic shape, wholly or partially, just as the development of the piece requires.

The chords in Example (a), p. 65, are each made out of three notes which follow one another in the retrograde inversion of the fourteen-note series.

The same method of alteration may be seen in the harmonic as in the melodic form of the series (Examples (a) and (c) ); individual notes appear transposed one or more octaves up or down, with the result that, instead of the original interval between them and the notes which precede or follow them in the series, the complementary interval appears—for instance, a major sixth instead of a minor third; only the tritone (augmented fourth or diminished fifth) remains the same. We simply note this possibility for the present, and will come back to explain its effects in detail in the next chapter. This increases the flexibility of the series from the compositional point of view in both the horizontal and vertical dimensions, without breaking the law of the fixed sequence of the notes in the series, and of the "relationship of notes only to one another". The same applies to the repetition of notes, which may take place without further ado; as, for instance, in bar 28, the G is heard on the fourth quaver in the 'cello and on the fifth in the viola. This is a *repetition* of a note, in the same or another instrument, which corresponds to a held note of equal length to the repeated notes, and is naturally possible. This differs from *going back to* a note, which is to be avoided. This occurs when a note is heard again after one or more other notes, but before all the remaining eleven notes have been heard, either horizontally or vertically.

The transposition of notes into another octave, and their immediate repetition, considerably enlarge the flexibility of the series, as required by the melodic line of the musical conception, or by the character of an individual part or figure, or as required for

70

general reasons connected with the kind of writing and the sonority aimed at. The inspiration alone is decisive in each case.

Further examples of the relation between the series and the general musical development are shown in the following extracts from the third of the Five Piano Pieces, Op. 23. Its "basic shape" consists of five notes and dominates the musical organisation of

the piece, which is thirty-five bars long and is written in a very virtuoso manner in all respects. Note the imitative repetition of the basic shape at the fifth above; this begins in the left hand with the note F, acting like a *comes*. Let us note the characteristic motifs contained in the basic shape: a leap of a sixth, and two parallel steps of a second separated by the leap of a fourth. These, together with their mirror forms (inversion, retrograde and retrograde inversion) produce many varying arrangements and relations of notes, from which a wealth of different shapes arise.

Bar 8 below shows, in contrast to Example (a) from the Serenade, the formation of chords by means of three contrapuntally treated parts which begin simultaneously in the right hand.

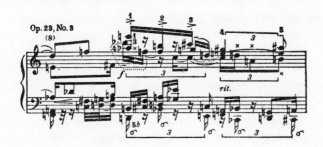

Each part starts the basic shape on a different note. However, these three notes, G—D flat—A flat, are not chosen arbitrarily, but are the first, third and fourth notes of the basic shape, which here appears as the upper part as well as in the form of a chord: G—B—C sharp (D flat)—G sharp (A flat)—A sharp (B flat). The basic shape is transposed here, but wherever it appears, either chordally or in a linear manner, it obeys the "Principle of the Intervals"; that is to say, the intervals in it always remain the same, not only in name, but in actual size too. We know this principle from polyphonic music, where in strict writing it is prescribed for the answer of a fugue subject in the so-called hexachord; the treatment of the series in twelve-note music has many other similarities to strict contrapuntal writing.

In bar 8 the left hand plays the second note B of the basic shape which is missing in the right hand, but with it, rather surprisingly, it plays not A sharp but D. The explanation of this change can be found in bar 2; there, after the fourth note of the basic shape in the right hand, the left hand begins an imitative repetition of the basic shape starting on F, i.e. on the fifth of the original entry on B flat. Just the same thing happens in bar 8; the D in the left hand begins the transposition of the basic shape at the fifth in the bass part, but here it appears simultaneously with the upper part which corresponds to it, not in imitation as in bar 2. The "mistake" in the order of the first two notes in the bass (D—B flat instead of B flat—D) is corrected by the remaining notes, (B flat—D)—E— C flat (B)—C sharp, so that one can call it a variant of the basic shape, with its first two notes exchanged. This example shows how imaginative the treatment of the series can be. In addition we shall see in the later course of the piece that this "irregularity", by which the interval of the sixth in the basic shape separates itself somewhat from the other notes, has definite musical consequences and thereby loses its seeming arbitrariness (one of many parallels in classical music is the C sharp in Brahms' Handel Variations mentioned on p. 49).

The next example shows (1) the possibilities of varying a musical shape by changing the pitch of the individual notes in the series,

and (2) some of the many variants which are possible within the five-note group; the notes are shaken up together—here within the set space of the accompaniment figure in the left hand—so that they produce various groupings of elements which appear simultaneously or consecutively and thereby are also able to change their order in the series. Thus in Group x the fifth note comes before the fourth note, in Group y the fourth before the third, in Group z the fourth before the second and third. But this is certainly not a purely intellectual jigsaw puzzle with notes, but a presentation of the *musical* relations in the structure of the basic shape.

Y and z are based on the two steps of a second which appear in the basic shape, together with their inversions. The interval of the sixth is fixed like a static pole, round which the three remaining notes rotate; one can either regard this sixth, as in y, as an inversion going upwards, with its continuation B—E—D following it, or we can make it go downwards, C sharp—F, with G—D—E as the continuation. There is the same "play" between w and x, here round the sixth F—A, or A—F. The upwards step of a second, F sharp—G sharp, in w is answered by the downwards step A flat—G flat (= G sharp—F sharp); in order to create a contrast by the change in direction of a motif, x has A flat—G flat, that is to say, the fifth note before the fourth, instead of G flat—A flat, which would be "correct", and would be possible without any difficulty through the mechanical "unrolling" of the series. But then it would not be right or purposive *musically*. One can also see that the note F is the common starting-point and pivot of the four note-groups in the left hand, the note B flat (its lower fifth) has the same function in the four note-groups in the right hand. So this is another application of the law which was established in the first bars of the piece with the basic shape and its "answer" at the fifth.

We will end this chapter with an interesting example from Op. 23, No. 3, its six-bar cadential final passage. It is interesting, because (1) one can see that here too, without any preconceived doctrinaire speculation, the development of the music is moving towards dodecaphony; and (2) this development fully conforms with the traditional classical principles of form. Let us consider the means with which a coda in tonal music fulfils its function, that of ending the development of the music. The music is still in motion, but is merely running to its end, and nothing is really happening; the actual development is marking time. To put it roughly, this is carried out by means of several repetitions of a concluding shape, which is simultaneously reduced in extent, harmonically it goes towards the tonic, with which it ends.

The following example from non-tonal music shows, with unsurpassable flexibility and clarity, a parallel case which completely corresponds to the classical procedure.

The concluding idea A here consists of the five-note basic shape and its imitative repetition from the beginning of the piece; but not in a linear form, as it is there—they are brought together vertically in two chords; the petals are closing.

Two points should be noticed:

1.   The division of the five notes into a four-note chord and a note after the beat. This separation has a parallel in the linear form in bar 2 of the piece, where the first note of the imitative repetition is inserted between the fourth and fifth notes of the basic shape. Further, the four-note chord also corresponds to that on the second crotchet of bar 8, in that the fifth note is isolated—a further musical relationship which has the effect of creating a connection with the passage in bar 8 and gives it a new and additional meaning and logic.

2.   The two notes which come after the beat, and are therefore accentuated, form a perfect fifth, C sharp (D flat)—F sharp. They are contrasted with the fifth C—G, which is heard like a pedal point up to the end of the piece and stands in the "leading-note" relation to C sharp—F sharp. This C and G also complement the ten different notes in the chords a and b to make twelve. Thus the original grouping of notes, 5 + 5, has become 5 + 5 + 2, and this becomes 4 + 4 + 4—a twelve-note series divided within itself.

75

$A_1$ repeats A *in situ*, doubly connected by the pedal point C—G; there is a slight variation, which corresponds to a harmonic variant of the same degree of the scale in tonal music; the basic shape, compressed into a chord, inverts itself round the fixed pivot of the sixth D—B flat, which is common to both a and $a_1$.

Similarly $b_1$ is a mirror-inversion round the sixth A—F of b. Bar 32 contains a—$a_1$—a, bar 33 (left hand) b—$b_1$—b, as a spatially reduced repetition of A + $A_1$ in a different arrangement of the material (variation!). Bars 34–35 then end with a further reduction on to the chord a.

The harmonic logic of these six bars becomes doubly clear if one draws a parallel with tonal music:

$$a\text{-}b/a_1\text{-}b_1\text{-}/a\text{-}a_1\text{-}a/b\text{-}b_1\text{-}b/a/a//$$
$$\text{I-V}/\text{I-V} / \quad \text{I} \quad / \quad \text{V} \quad /\text{I}/\text{I}//$$

The analytical extracts from Schoenberg's Op. 23 and 24 which we have made all show a common characteristic feature: all the harmonic and melodic formations in a piece or movement have arisen from one and the same sequence of notes. This note-sequence or series, both in the number of notes it contains, and in the intervals which they form with one another, is, as a melodic element, part of the conception which is the foundation of the piece; i.e. the basic shape. This, both as a whole and also in its melodic, rhythmical and formal components, contains all the characteristic features from which the content and character of the piece are formed (put together or composed) and developed.

This clarifies and justifies the rôle which the series, as the given melodic extract of the "basic shape", plays as a factor which creates shape, form and coherence in the musical organisation of the piece in question; this rôle corresponds to that of tonality or of a key. Just as in a tonal piece each note always has a direct or indirect relationship to the key-note, so here in every position it is always part of a series. For, as we have seen, everything is derived from the series—chords, main and subsidiary parts, accompanying figures, etc. This presupposes (or, one could say, it follows from this) that the series must be present in every moment of the course of the music; in other words, it must be continually repeated. Thus the requirement that the series must be repeated without cessation arises from a *musical* necessity.

Serial composition in the works mentioned above led to a perpetual and close interplay between the motivic (thematic), melodic and rhythmical fields of force; this interplay despised a mere mechanical "unrolling" of the series, and instead completely fused it into the musical "play" of notes, figures and forms.

We have already learnt some of the results of this interplay, from the point of view of the technique of composition, by means of the examples in this chapter. Schoenberg was next able to transfer them to twelve-note composition without further ado; for this was merely the final consequence of what had developed in the form of serial composition in Op. 23 and 24, from the law given by the basic musical conception. Twelve-note composition first appeared at the moment when Schoenberg used all the twelve notes of our tempered system in the basic shape, and, as a result, in the series. This only corresponded to the general tendency of music towards dodecaphony which we have been able to demonstrate in his works and those of various other composers after 1900. Thus this final decisive step, too, was not the result of intellectual speculation, but of the "hearing-out" and perception of an actual musical development; this development proved at the same time, that twelve-note ideas could be invented unconsciously by means of creative intuition, and did not need to be "constructed". This was in the late summer of 1921. On 1 December, 1923, Schoenberg wrote to J. M. Hauer: "... *This has been my position for about two years, and I must acknowledge that up till now I have not yet found any mistake in it—the first time this has happened—and that the system grows under my hands without my doing anything to it: I think this is a good sign. Through it I am completely in the position of being able to compose as unhesitatingly and imaginatively as one only does in one's youth and yet I remain under a precisely definable aesthetic control.*[8]

## CHAPTER VI

## Composition With Twelve Notes

*I. The derivation of a twelve-note series from the basic
shape—Essence and function of the twelve-note series
—The principle of the intervals—The four forms
of a twelve-note series—The principle of the co-
ordination of the vertical and the horizontal dimensions in music*

*II. The twelve-note series in practical composition*

SCHOENBERG'S discovery of the twelve-note series was
of fundamental importance from two points of view: firstly for the
new ordering, which had now become a necessity, of the material
of sound which had no tonal centre, and secondly for the unity
and ordering of the development of non-tonal music in the
line of the classical and pre-classical tradition.

At the moment when it was no longer possible to relate
harmonic and melodic phenomena to a key-note, they lost an
essential basis of their musical and logical coherence. From then
on—and not the other way round—the material of music perforce
reached a crisis; for with the cessation of tonality the ordering
of the notes produced by tonality—harmonically by means of
the triad, and melodically by means of the major and minor
scales—no longer applied. This tonal organisation is a hierarchy,
set up and ruled over by the key-note, which drew all the remaining eleven notes towards itself, and related them to itself. They
only existed through the key-note, as its satellites; as being the
third, sixth, etc., of the key-note. The method of figured bass
shows this "ordering through subordination" at its clearest.
This subordination, and the relations and possibilities of the
combination of notes with one another which had been compre-

hensively arranged in this way, had impressed themselves more and more on the subconsciousness of the composer as time went on, so that his imagination soon used them unconsciously and intuitively. But this unconscious use of the material which was based on a tonal centre gradually led—especially where the power of custom overcame that of the creative imagination—to a kind of "ossification" of certain sequences of notes; this increasingly led to the formation of turns of harmony and melody which came readily to hand and had the character of formulae. Where a real creative instinct exploded these arrangements of notes (which had become conventional) and discovered new ones, it had the effect of abolishing the subordination of the notes to a key-note as well as their derivation from it; this led to the dissolution of tonality. The crisis in the material of music, which was thus caused by a creative process, was compelling and productive *musically* (that was why it took place)—not intellectually, but only because of a creative process which was mirrored in the musical organisation of a work: through a *conception*.

Composition with twelve notes related only to one another again sets note against note in consciousness of the material, and in fulfilment of an order imposed upon the material by music; for in the shape of the twelve-note series it gives back each note its own musical weight, its inherent meaning and its individuality; these had been lost under the dictatorship of tonality. (There even a change of key-note meant only a shift in parallel of the tonal relations, which had become static.) This method also retains the individuality of the note, or, more accurately, it keeps on renewing it; for in twelve-note composition the ordering of the musical material is not *a priori*, nor static and always remaining the same, but is dynamic and changes from work to work. First the basic conception (which is thematic) has to choose the order of the twelve notes in the series; it arranges the order which fits it, i.e. the one that serves it best. According to this the notes "get into series"—a different one for each piece —and are ready for the composition. Here the notes are still "related only to one another" (instead of being related to one key-note only, as before), and these interval-relations between the notes, which are determined by the series, vary according to the law of the original conception which called them into being; so does the series, which is implicit in the basic conception and is derived from it.

If the idea of the composer is realised in the basic conception and its working out in practice, then each note gets back its own individuality—till the conception of the next work. Thus, in contrast to the system of tonality, which was static, or at any rate became static, twelve-note composition contains a dynamic principle for the ordering of its material. This musical order depends on the twelve-note series, which has to be invened anew for each work in the form of a thematic conception. This musical coherence defines the second function of the note-series as an element in the presentation and development of musical ideas and forms: as a result of its provenance from the basic shape, the first creative thought, the twelve-note series represents the preliminary melodic formation of the whole thematic material of the work.

This double function, of being responsible for the ordering of the musical material and of forming the thematic material in advance, gives the twelve-note series, working in conjunction with the traditional means of composition, a pivotal importance. Its practical effects and consequences will be systematically examined in the following pages—starting with the series itself—and the uses of these in composition will be summarised.

*The method of composing with twelve tones grew out of the necessity . . . of creating a new procedure in musical construction which seemed fitted to replace those formal and structural differences provided formerly by tonal harmonies. This method consists primarily of the constant and exclusive use of a set of twelve different tones. This means, of course, that no tone is repeated within the series and that it uses all twelve tones of the chromatic scale, though in a different order.*[2]

Such a twelve-note series is undefined rhythmically, and follows the "principle of the intervals": the intervals built out of the note-sequence of the basic thematic conception are unalterable in size within the series.

We already know this principle from the laws of contrapuntal writing, according to which a fugue theme (*dux*) had to be answered in the so-called hexachord, in order to fulfil the requirement that the *comes* must contain the same intervals as the *dux*, not only in name but in actual size.

The "principle of the intervals" applies to all the four forms in which the series can appear: (1) the original—O; (2) its inversion—I, which arises from the inversion of all the intervals of the original; (3) the retrograde—R, which begins with the twelfth note of the original and runs back to the first; and (4) the inversion of the retrograde—RI.

These are different forms of one and the same melodic sequence —through the conception of "musical space" it can be viewed from different directions—they correspond to one another fully in their melodic structure, and they are of equal musical importance (compare the horizontal section, vertical section and cross-section in geometry).

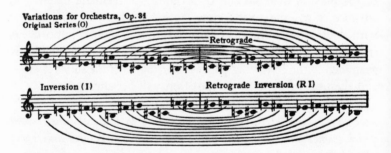

The use of these mirror forms was a commonplace among the masters of the polyphonic age of music; in J. S. Bach's last works, the "Art of Fugue" and the "Musical Offering", they often determine the entire musical development, and Beethoven also used them in his last creative period.

In order to be able to compose freely and unconstrainedly, in spite of all the strictness of the law of the series, it had to be possible to use the notes of a series and its mirror forms as freely as the musical imagination demanded: the law had to be capable of being followed strictly but handled freely.

Here the second principle comes in, that of the co-ordination between vertical and horizontal phenomena in music. This also corresponds to the concept of the unity of the musical space:

*The elements of a musical idea are partly incorporated in the horizontal plane as successive sounds, and partly in the vertical plane as simultaneous sounds. The mutual relation of tones regulates the succession of intervals as well as their association into harmonies; the rhythm regulates the succession of tones as well as the succession of harmonies, and organises phrasing.*[2]

We also find this co-ordination of melody and harmony in classical tonal music, as well as in modern music. In practical composition it takes this form: the notes of a melody (and the intervals which form it) may also be combined to form chords, wholly or partially, separately or in groups. Then the interval-steps in the melody also appear as harmonic intervals in the chords. This also means that the twelve notes of a series, which presents the melodic element of the basic conception, can be used (a) as a unit or (b) separately or (c) in groups in both the horizontal and vertical dimensions, as the inspiration of the music demands.

(a) Schoenberg, Fourth String Quartet, Op. 37, first movement:

(b) *Op. cit.*, third movement:

(c) *Op. cit.*, first movement:

We will now give in summary form the following rules and directions for twelve-note composition: their practical application will be shown later with examples from Schoenberg's works.

1. *Structure of a series* A twelve-note series consists of the twelve different notes of our tempered system; they come in the sequence ordained by the primary musical conception, the basic shape. No note is repeated within the series.

2. *Mirror forms of a series* Schoenberg's method consists of the continuous and exclusive repetition of a series of twelve

notes. Each series can be used in four forms which are of equal musical value (i.e. as regards their content)—the original form and its three mirror forms: inversion, retrograde and retrograde inversion. Each of the four forms can be linked with itself or with any one of the other three forms, either consecutively or simultaneously.

It is well known that symmetry has an extremely important function in creating shape and form in music. We can think of the fundamental symmetry of the harmonic structure of a theme and a movement, and especially of symmetrically built types of themes, in which the stress is not so much on equal distance from the axis of symmetry as on the presence of the axis itself. The axis separates, i.e. divides, and also holds the theme together. So far as I know, no one has yet discussed the powerful effect of these symmetrical relations on the creation of form—those in the horizontal (melodic) dimension, between the original series and its retrograde and between inversion and retrograde inversion; and those in the vertical (contrapuntal) dimension, between original series and inversion and between retrograde and retrograde inversion. But this seems to be of great, if not fundamental importance for musical coherence. In practice Schoenberg's themes contain combinations of symmetrically corresponding forms of the series in such a way that, for instance, the consequent in the horizontal dimension mostly uses the retrograde of the series of the antecedent, while in the vertical dimension—which turns round an axis of symmetry which is here thought of as being horizontal—the inversion is predominant. This shows the unconscious logic of his feeling for form.

3. *Use of the series or its notes in the horizontal and vertical dimensions* The twelve notes of a series can appear either

(a) Only horizontally, i.e. purely as a melody, or

(b) Only vertically, combined in one or more chords, or

(c) They can be divided, either individually or in groups, between the main part and the accompaniment (whether the latter consists of chords, figurations or subsidiary parts), or else between several contrapuntal parts.

This division will also show or cause a musical "motivation", as a rule (first movement of the fourth String Quartet).

The following examples of the use of the series in actual composition may also be found in Schoenberg's works:

4. *Transpositions of a twelve-note series* Each of the four forms of the series may be transposed on to any one of the remaining eleven notes of the chromatic scale: this produces forty-eight series altogether. These transpositions function in a similar manner to modulations in tonal music, and thus serve to create subsidiary (e.g. transitional) ideas.

5. *Change of octave pitch—formation of complementary intervals* Each note can appear within the series in any octave upwards or downwards. From this alteration in the pitch of an individual note there arise the intervals which are complementary to the original ones in respect of the notes on each side of it.

This alteration of the pitch of a note results from its relative independence within the series, its inherent meaning, which has already been discussed in detail. The following example from No. 9 of J. S. Bach's three-part Inventions shows that an alteration in pitch of this kind has always been musically possible;

This shows a case where notes are transposed into the lower octave in a regular pattern; from this the complementary intervals result. It seems likely that this procedure is related to the methods of double counterpoint, which produces a variation of the vertical sound of the music, and thus a development in the music itself, by transposing a part into a higher or lower octave.

6. *Repetition of notes* The rule of the twelve-note series allows no repetition of notes within the series. But, just as in strict contrapuntal writing, one must understand the concept of note-repetition in a *musical* sense here, i.e. as the too early return of a note, which is therefore conspicuous. Contrapuntal technique recommended the avoidance of this, or at any rate recommended that the note which returned should be quitted in the opposite direction from that in which it was approached, in order to make its too early return less conspicuous and to gloss it over.

In contrast to this, *immediate* repetitions of notes are just as possible and practical in twelve-note music as they are in contrapuntal writing:

(a) As a characteristic element in a musical idea.

(b) For reasons connected with instrumental technique or on grounds of sonority—if a note which is to be held for a fairly long time is liable to stop sounding too soon (e.g. piano, string pizzicato, plucked and percussion instruments).

(c) For compositional reasons, e.g. a pedal point (see Table XIV U between pages 214 and 215).

(a)

(b)

(b) and (e)

To this category also belong (d) trills and (e) tremolos.
(d) Fourth Quartet, third movement.

(f)

(g)

Accompaniment figures (f) and repetitions of groups of notes (g) are to be regarded in a similar way to the repetitions of notes in (b), as chords which are struck again or repeated several times at short intervals for reasons of sonority or because of the instruments involved. Finally, the Ostinato also belongs to the category of the repetitions of notes which are possible; its musical function can be regarded as that of a "melodic pedal-point" (Table XII R, bars 636-7; Example f, p. 89: Table XVI M).

7. *Avoidance of octave doubling*   In his music Schoenberg avoids any doubling of notes at the octave. *To double is to emphasise, and an emphasised tone could be interpreted as a root, or even a tonic; the consequences of such an interpretation must be avoided.*[2] Schoenberg recommended the avoidance of octave doublings even in his *Harmonielehre*, which appeared in 1911, at a time when twelve-note composition did not exist. Thus one can interpret this both as a peculiarity of Schoenberg's style and as a sign of the inherent logic of his musical imagination, which already unconsciously obeyed a principle of twelve-note music; his imagination was clearly turning towards it long in advance. Perhaps the prohibition of octave doublings could be compared with that of parallel octaves in tonal music. In any case, Schoenberg's instinctive avoidance of octave doublings became a law to him. But, like all purposive restrictions of compositional freedom in obedience to a law, it had a positive effect elsewhere; for it is connected with other constructive aims which lead to varied subdivisions of the series and to the separation of the notes into groups; this lead to a "differentiation" which heightens the elasticity of the series for the purpose of composition and, above all, expands and refines its powers of creating form. This will be frequently discussed later on. A clear distinction must be drawn between this kind of octave doubling, which arises from "impure" part-writing, and that sort of octave doubling which is consciously used purely for reasons of sonority; for instance the latter appears throughout the "Ode to Napoleon", Op. 41, as a characteristic element of the style (Table XV ff.).

8. *Subdivision of a series—formation of note-groups*   A series can be subdivided one or more times—into two groups of six notes each, three of four notes, or four of three notes. There can

also be other subdivisions, as, for instance, in the first movement of the third String Quartet, Op. 30. There, besides the subdivision into antecedent and consequent, there is also one into 5+5+2 notes; this stands in a direct relation to the new forms in this movement.

An interesting case can be found in the Ode, Op. 41. There the series first appears in a chord-group made up of tonal triads. Later in the course of the work, the chordal structure of this group allows the most varied melodic combinations to be derived from it; from these the original series emerges more and more clearly. The original series is then not only divided into six-, four- and three-note groups, but, thanks to the peculiar "leading-note" relation of the sequence of triads which forms its basis, it is actually divided into two-note groups, made up entirely of minor seconds separated by thirds (Table XV B[1]).

The purpose and effects of the subdivision of the series vary considerably. The subdivision into two sections of six notes each—the antecedent and consequent of the series—gives a basis for alterations of a quite definite kind (see p. 92). Division into two or more groups makes the series easier to handle; this is especially necessary in works which are contrapuntally constructed, for long-drawn-out melodic phrases are unsuitable for contrapuntal treatment, which demands relatively short thematic structures, like fugue subjects.

Division into groups also makes it possible to regard these as small independent series and to treat them as such; they remain unaltered in themselves, but can change places with one another. This is especially convincing from the musical point of view when the same interval comes more than once in the twelve-note series (e.g. the diminished fifth in the series of Op. 25) and thus creates an interval-relation between the groups, which allows them to be exchanged. The important effects on form of the actual formation of the groups will be discussed in another connection.

9. *The invention of a twelve-note series,* (a) *As a musical conception.*

*The first conception of a series always takes place in the form of a thematic character.*[9] This means that Schoenberg obtains the twelve-note series from the musical conception which is the first creative idea of a work; the sequence of the notes is formed by this.

We have already frequently mentioned this fact, which is essential to Schoenberg's twelve-note composition. It is underlined by the fact that—as we have been able to show—twelve-note melodies or themes can arise unconsciously as musical ideas, and that these are found in the works of many different composers. Both these facts decisively weaken all the allegations that twelve-note music in general, and Schoenberg's works in particular, are primarily the result of a purely intellectual process.

We should note that Schoenberg speaks, not of a "theme", but of a "thematic character". The latter is more all-embracing, and means that the original musical idea can, but need not, be a complete theme. "Thematic character" does not define the form or set any limits; it can mean a musical shape or only a part of a shape. If we think of Richard Strauss' remark, quoted on p. 57, and of the analysis of Beethoven's Op. 10, No. 1, then as a rule we can equate this first unconscious conception with what we called the basic shape. *The latter is the basic conception:* it already contains the series within itself as a melodic element, and everything else is invented and shaped from it. Conception, invention and shaping thus seem to be the three complementary forms of the creative process. (This fundamental distinction between conception and invention exactly corresponds to the remarks which Stravinsky has made in his *Poétique Musicale*.)

Naturally the identification of the basic conception with the basic shape in relation to twelve-note music is not to be understood in any dogmatic or exclusive way; it is an instructive and orientating explanation of a musical fact which is of frequent occurrence. In Schoenberg's works we find series both in the form of basic shapes and also contained in thematic ideas which cannot be simply regarded as basic shapes: for instance the beginning of the Piano Piece, Op. 33a, which first of all states the series in the form of three four-part chords,

or the extremely instructive contrast to this, the basic group of chords out of which the Ode, Op. 41, is formed (Table XV B), and the first of the Six Male Voice Choruses, Op. 35, in which the series is first contained in a five-bar contrapuntal formation, and appears for the first (and only) time in linear form in the twenty-third bar of the piece, which is only thirty bars long (Table XVII A, B). The introduction to the Variations for Orchestra, Op. 31, shows a specially interesting case, which is worth detailed study from the point of view of the development of the music. In the thirty-three bars of the introduction and corresponding in this to its formal purpose the twelve-note series of the work, together with its mirror forms, gradually grows from a note to an interval, from an interval to a group of notes, until in bar 34 (the entry of the theme of the variations) it appears for the first time as a whole. We repeat: it is always the imagination, together with the musical conception, which sets the pace.

(b) *Constructed series* Departing from Schoenberg's practice, there also exists the possibility, which is frequently used to-day, of forming a twelve-note series by conscious construction. Anyone who has tried to "build" such a series even once will understand that even in this case a *musician* will not pursue a purely mathematical calculation, but will involuntarily ..low his imagination its play. The concept of "building" retains its suggestive function even when used as a conscious process, beginning from setting the first interval, and going on to the kind of continuation needed, the "melodic course", the subdivision of the series and other factors. This will make itself felt, unconsciously and unavoidably, in the work of one who is practised and experienced in musical thinking, as well as in that of a gifted beginner. Much that will be said below about alterations in a series, about corresponding intervals and about special subdivisions and methods of building a series will be of use in the creation of a twelve-note series by constructional methods. Composition with a series which is built in this way has parallels of several kinds, for instance in variations based on a theme by another composer, or in the composition of a fugue, the subject of which also consists of a "series" of notes, which have to be "built" in advance so as to be usable in double counterpoint, stretto, etc.

10. *Alterations in the series.*
*It will not often happen that one obtains a perfect series which is fit for use as the first immediate conception. A little working-over*

*afterwards is usually necessary. But the character of the piece is already present in the first form of the series. This working over depends chiefly on constructional considerations. For example I endeavour to avoid one of the forms ending with the same tone with which another begins, and vice versa, for fear of monotony. Personally I endeavour to keep the series such that the inversion of the first six tones a fifth lower gives the remaining six tones. The consequent, the seventh to twelfth tones, is a different sequence of these second six tones. This has the advantage that one can accompany melodic phrases made from the first six tones with harmonies made from the second six tones, without getting doublings.*[10]

Working-over is a matter of maturity and experience in composition. It demands both imagination which will foresee and perceive the work as a whole, and technical ability, in order to know where, why and how far working-over is necessary. Beethoven's sketch-books are still an inexhaustible compendium for this. The working out of motivic relationships, the co-ordination of a melody with its accompaniment, the removal of unevennesses which interrupt the flow of music, the reduction of too luxuriant subsidiary parts, the achievement of clear and plastic forms—all this and much more can be the object of working-over in composition, in tonal as well as in twelve-note music. It is mostly "constructional considerations" that arise. By the way, an excellent preparation for this is the carrying out of a good deal of practical writing of strict counterpoint, in which double and triple counterpoint, the working out of fugue subjects in stretto, chorale arrangements, etc., compel and educate the hand and mind from the beginning in undertaking working-over: for the laws of strict writing, too, are of a definitely "constructional" nature.

The "working-over" of the series mentioned by Schoenberg naturally brings with it a corresponding correction to the original conception; but its musical character is not thereby altered. The object is to make the series "perfect and fit for use". Example (c) on p. 84 shows the series of the fourth String Quartet and illustrates Schoenberg's remarks; the inversion of the first half of the series at the lower fifth contains the six notes of the second half, but in a different order; (naturally this also applies to the inversion of the second half in respect of the notes of the first half). This allows Schoenberg, for example, to use the original series and the inversion at the lower fifth simultaneously in bars 27–28 of the first movement of the fourth String Quartet (Table VI A). If the inversion of the series starting on D had been used here, it would have annulled the law of the series, as some notes (e.g. D sharp and C sharp in the first half of bar 27) would have been repeated too early, and in addition octave doublings (D, C, A flat at x and xx in the example below) would have arisen; this would have made the writing unclear.

In contrast to this the passage in the Quartet itself shows an extremely clear disposition which has a definite musical logic; the first and second violin parts come from the original series, the viola and 'cello from the inversion at the lower fifth. The parts are coupled in pairs, and present all the twelve notes horizontally and vertically in half-bar units by the combination of both pairs of parts. If it had been a question of one of the two forms of the series accompanying the other with chords, the result of our contrasting the two transpositions would have been still cruder. It is the purpose and task of working-over, among other things, to rule out such procedures in advance.

*Sometimes a set* (series) *will not fit every condition an experienced composer can foresee, especially in those ideal cases where the set appears at once in the form, character, and phrasing of a theme. Rectifications in the order of tones may then become necessary.*[2] From what has been said above it is easy to understand what Schoenberg means here.

As a marginal note, we may mention here a peculiarity of Schoenberg's series, without discussing whether it is accidental or expresses a law. As we have said, Schoenberg arranges the inversion of the series in such a way that, while observing definite mutual note-relations with the original series, the former begins a fifth below. This relation of a fifth between the first notes of each series clearly corresponds to an acoustical law of nature— that between a note and its strongest and most frequent overtone —and perhaps the fact that the inversion starts a fifth lower than the original shows Schoenberg's endeavour to express a law in the choice of the first notes of the two series too. Similar tendencies can already be found in his earlier twelve-note compositions, for instance in the Wind Quintet, Op. 26 (Table III B). Here the notes of the antecedent and consequent of the original series stand in the relation of a perfect fifth to one another, up to the last two notes. On the other hand, as the Variations for Orchestra, Op. 31, show, the note-relations which are required may be arrived at by other transpositions than that to the lower fifth, so that one can see more in the choice of the fifth, to which Schoenberg finally came, than a technical accident.

11. *Corresponding intervals and note-groups*  We have already pointed out that the presence of two intervals of equal size within a series can, in certain circumstances, not only produce or suggest a definite subdivision of the series, but, when a series is divided into groups—which, as we have said, can also be used as small independent series—also allows these groups to be exchanged with one another. Schoenberg mentions the Suite, Op. 25, the series of which has a diminished fifth between its third and fourth notes and between its seventh and eighth notes. The division into three four-note groups resulting from this makes it

possible to couple these groups together, both horizontally and vertically, to allow them to overlap one another, and finally to introduce the second group before the first at the beginning of the Minuet.

It should be noted that in a case like this the same correspondence of intervals as in the original series naturally also applies to all its mirror forms and transpositions. For example, if one simultaneously uses two forms of the series which are so placed that they both contain the same interval, here D flat—G and G sharp —D,

one can use this common interval as a vertical sound and then contrast it with the remaining notes of both groups, which are now joined into a new combination of notes. In Op. 31 the original series actually has four intervals in common with its inversion a diminished fifth lower.

With a little imagination one can see from these examples the countless possibilities of related combinations of notes for the purpose of creating forms.

The division of a series into an antecedent and consequent of six notes each is another matter. In the Fantasy for Violin and Piano, Op. 47, what appears at the beginning to be the complete original series soon turns out to be only a coupling of its antecedent with its inversion a fifth lower; this inversion also contains the remaining six notes of the consequent, but in a different order. The consequent, i.e. the second half of the series, first appears in bar 10, again independently and combined with its own inversion. In other words, Schoenberg treats the antecedent and consequent from the outset as two independent six-note series (Table XVIII).

This naturally has consequences for the formal development. It is easy to see that, in comparison with a twelve-note series, a six-note one, from the nature of the material, limits the thematic invention to figures of shorter length and therefore also of less richness in thematic shapes. Now if—to look at the other side —a composer, as in the present case, wishes to write a relatively short piece of ten minutes' duration, his sense of form will make him see to it in advance that the richness of the thematic material is in conformity with the form of the whole piece, and this includes its length. The form of a work depends on its content. A composer's thought will create form logically and will obey the law of artistic economy; therefore he will instinctively try to present the content as exhaustively as possible. This means, from the other point of view, that he will not bring in any musical ideas which are superfluous or would cause the content to "overflow" the form. He will not bring in anything which one *could* either leave out or take out afterwards; rather it is what one *has* to leave out in order not to overburden the content and form, or spoil its clarity and perspective. This is an indispensable law for every work of art.

From this we can again see how close is the organic connection of the series with the other elements of composition, especially the creation of form; and also how sensitively the musical organism not only reacts to every musical "impulse" which is seemingly merely of local importance, but is indeed continually influenced by conditions arising from the musical material, i.e. the series. The more subtle a composer's feeling for form is, the richer musical harvest he will be able to obtain from the series. The more familiar he is with its use, the more freely and unconstrictedly he will be able to compose, whether it be a short song or an opera which lasts a whole evening.

Many composers use two or even more twelve-note series in the same work—a development of Schoenberg's idea which we will discuss later. But his Op. 47, with its two six-note series, perhaps points out the solution of many problems which the use of more than one series raises. Above all, the problem of unity, which Schoenberg completely solved through the use of only one series, is the central point. In Op. 47 the law of the series is handled in such a varied manner that two series arise out of one—a most imaginative conception—with all the musical and especially all the formal consequences of such duality, but also with the possibility of becoming a unity again, if the musical thought demands. And perhaps this "play" between the two series here is itself a part of the development, just as the development is part of the whole idea of the piece; but this would be a *musical* effect caused by the series itself. We shall discuss later the functions of the series in creating form, as shown in Op. 47.

12.   *The interval-structure of the twelve-note series—specially constructed series*   Every twelve-note series consists of the twelve different notes of our tempered system, which can form at the most eleven intervals between them. As the series used by Schoenberg always came into being together with the first creative conception of a work, the kind and size of the intervals in the series in question was given at the same time by this. Any alterations there might be were mainly confined to the working out of certain *correspondences* of intervals for compositional reasons, and depended on the principle of repetition mentioned above; it is easy to see that a series gains in melodic coherence by the repetition of the same interval at different points within it, and that the relationship between note-groups formed from a series of this kind (as has already been shown in connection with Op. 25) will be heightened thereby; and also that the series' power of creating form—its most essential function—will be strengthened.

Last but not least, the repetition of one or more intervals

within the series will increase the melodic comprehensibility of the music, to the listener, from the melodic point of view, and will facilitate its study for the performer, especially for the singer.

If, following Schoenberg's procedure, we leave out octave doublings, the twelve notes can form up to eleven different intervals, from the minor second to the major seventh. As it is possible to transpose a note in the series to other octave pitches, the complementary interval can arise (see p. 86); this is used for melodic variation. The diminished fifth alone has a special position, for its complementary interval, when the octave pitch is altered, is still the same diminished fifth. The unalterability of this interval allows the diminished fifth to be used, both within the series and in interplay with the mirror forms, as a "pivot" interval, by means of which the note-groups can be exchanged with one another, or one series can leap over into another. We saw a starting-point of this in the third Piece of Op. 23 (see p. 73). This creates close melodic connections between the different forms of the series, but can also easily obliterate or remove their differences from one another, which are so important for melodic variation.

Further, a series may be condensed melodically (a) if a sequence of two or three intervals is repeated within the series, as the alternative consequents of the series (Cons$_2$, Cons$_3$) show in the following example. This needs no further explanation. Or (b) if the series is constructed symmetrically. In the basic type of a symmetrical series the six-note consequent is a mirror form (inversion, retrograde or retrograde inversion) of the antecedent.

10

Our example shows how a symmetrical series can be built. First the antecedent of the original series is invented as a melodic progression, combined contrapuntally with its inversion a fifth lower; following Schoenberg's tendency, this contains the remaining six notes of the series, i.e. those belonging to the consequent. But while, as a rule, the consequent of the original series contains the notes of the inversion at the lower fifth in a different order (e.g. as in Cons$_4$), it is here the retrograde inversion of the antecedent. This ensures complete symmetry between both halves of the series, and further makes the following forms of the whole series and its mirror forms identical. The inversion at the lower fifth is also the retrograde of the original series, and the retrograde of the inversion at the lower fifth is again the original series itself. But this means that the four possible forms of a series have been reduced to two—here the original and the inversion at the lower fifth; this is a considerable unification of the melodic element, not without an equally considerable restriction of the possibilities of melodic expansion and variation. Further, as each half of the series is melodically exactly similar to the other half, it means that we really only have a six-note series with its inversion a fifth lower, as the consequents are both only transpositions of the antecedents; thus the number of possible melodic and harmonic arrangements of the notes will be again halved in practice.

The series of Op. 41 (see Table XV B1) is also symmetrical. Here the consequent is simply a transposition of the antecedent, so that here too one can speak of a six-note series. The antecedent itself is again symmetrical, as its last three notes are the retrograde inversion of the first three. This double symmetry has the consequence that the inversion and retrograde inversion of the series are the same as the original and retrograde forms respectively; but the places of the antecedent and consequent are exchanged in each case.

Let us here try to draw an interesting parallel which shows the connection with musical tradition, and may perhaps therefore be of practical use. Just as in the thematic "sentence" form in classical music the consequent represents a consequence and further development of the antecedent, just as in the fugue the counter-subject is a consequence of the subject which precedes it and is so built as to be combined with it, so in the twelve-note series the antecedent is the primary, dominating and more important part of the series. The consequent has to content itself with the remaining six notes, and must also fit in with the antecedent; the position is the same in the musical conception, both in twelve-note music and in tonal music: the consequent is already a consequence from the preceding antecedent.

Other specially constructed series are: (a) *The so-called "all-interval series"* This contains all the eleven possible intervals, none of them being repeated. From what has been said above, it follows that this series will produce the vaguest melodic connections, together with extreme melodic richness. But it at once becomes clear that the latter is only relative, when we think of the "double" nature of the interval and its complementary "mirror form". Allowing for this, only six intervals at the most are feasible: minor second—major seventh, major second—minor seventh, minor third—major sixth, major third—minor sixth, perfect fourth—perfect fifth and the diminished fifth. If one continues in the same direction, the same interval-relationships are repeated, but in reverse order. Regarded in this way, the series given above contains all the six possible intervals, but with a much more stable melodic structure and with interval-relations which are musically more fertile.

(b) *Series with tonal "colouring"* These are series which consist wholly or partly of elements of tonal triads (major, minor or augmented), or of sequences of such triads. The latter is the case with Schoenberg's Op. 41, which has already been mentioned several times; it ends with a pure chord of E flat major, though no feeling of a key-note arises during the course of the piece. It is therefore more correct to speak, not of a triad of E flat, but of a triad consisting of the notes E flat—G—B flat, which gradually emerges—prepared for and yet surprising—in the course of the musical development out of the melodic and harmonic play of the twelve notes. Thus this is really a pure twelve-note composition after all.

One of the first cases of a series built out of broken tonal triads is that of Alban Berg's Violin Concerto:

This series mainly consists of an intertwined chain of major and minor triads. Berg also used a similar procedure in his opera "Lulu", without circumventing the law of Schoenberg's serial composition in either case. For the sake of completeness it should be added that the three diminished seventh chords and also the four augmented triads contain between them all the twelve notes of the scale.

What has been said here about the "working-over" of a twelve-note series and·its computable constructional possibilities—or rather, necessities—should be regarded and treated from two different points of view, as is the case with the rules and instructions of counterpoint or the classical technique of composition. For composition exercises, in which the student has to search for difficulties consciously and resolve them consciously, they only serve as a guide and a means of stimulation. Here he can never do too much of a good thing. But for artistic creation the position is different. Here the composer's imagination must select, control and direct, so that—to take an example—the working out of melodic correspondences in the series does not degenerate into an intellectual game and thus lose sight of the higher musical necessities, which should always have the first and last word. Otherwise there is a danger of aridity and monotony; in the case mentioned above these can easily arise from the restriction of the content of the series and of the possibilities of variation which this content allows.

13. *The meaning of the twelve-note series for composition— athematic music—the use of two series—a new tonality* In connection with the increasing expansion of composition with twelve notes, two questions especially have arisen in practice about which the most opposing views have been expressed. One of them arose for the first time in the first decade of this century, in connection with the beginnings of non-tonal music. This was the problem of so-called athematic music; in the last decade it has apparently acquired a new importance in connection with twelve-note music. The other question concerns the simultaneous use of two or more twelve-note series in a composition.

The thesis of athematic music has been supported in recent years by some musicians in the following way: the use of the twelve-note series guarantees such security to the musical coherence of a piece that one can do without the means of thematic or motivic definition (both are essentially the same). Up to now it has not been explained if and in what form and shape such music can express thoughts, with what means and according to what laws. In any case Schoenberg unmistakably and expressly refused to bring his music into any connection with the concept of athematism. He had, indeed, maintained something of the kind for a short time about 1910, long before Alois Hába. *But I soon withdrew it, as coherence in music can only depend on motifs and their metamorphoses and developments.*[10]

Naturally one should not understand the concept of the motif from too narrow a point of view in this connection; a rhythm by itself (e.g. in the third movement of Berg's Chamber Concerto) or a certain sonority, among other things, can be regarded and treated as a motif, i.e. repeated several times during the course of a piece and thus have the effect of connecting the form. . . . *Not everything is not gold, which does not glitter, and something can be thematic which does not in the least look like it.*[10] We may add: and which the composer himself perhaps may not perceive as being thematic.

This may serve as the necessary clarification of the position, as far as Schoenberg and his composition with twelve notes are concerned. In any case no conclusion can be reached about all these problems through theoretical discussion, but only through actual works of art.

The same applies to the question whether one can use more than one series in a work. One can—of course. And whether it is a work of art or not will not depend on this. It will only depend, as in all other periods, on whether the music is good, whether it says anything to us, and how it says it. Nothing would be more contrary to the spirit of a master like Schoenberg, who all his life had to suffer, perhaps more than anyone else, from the dogmatic narrow-mindedness of professional musicians, than to make a dogma out of this question. We are not discussing here whether a composer uses two or more series in a work through ignorance or misunderstanding of Schoenberg's idea and method; or whether he is worried about his own independence and the individuality of the style of his music and therefore wants to do something different at all costs (as if individuality were a question of will-power). We are only interested in seeing if and how far the simultaneous use of two or more series corresponds to Schoenberg's idea and practice; that is to say, to his idea and method of making music: and if it does contradict them, what consequences result.

Schoenberg's own position is clear, both in his works and in his writings. He has corrected Leibowitz' remarks on this point*, as also those about athematism in his own music: . . . *so the supplementary half-series, which he adduces, is incorrect. Only in the third String Quartet, for fear of monotony, did I use two forms of the sequence of notes in the consequent of the series, while the antecedent, the first six notes, remains unaltered. It does not seem right to me to use more than one series, but nevertheless the main thing is whether the music is good. The principles according to which it is constructed are a matter of secondary or tertiary importance.*[10]

In other words, one can also make good music with two series, or without any series at all, as in the early non-tonal music; or on a tonal basis, whether based on functional harmony or on the new synthesis with the experiments in serial composition,

* *Introduction à la musique de douze sons*, Éditions L'Arche, Paris.

which was first used by Schoenberg, for instance in the Variations on a Recitative for Organ, Op. 40, or the Variations for Orchestra, Op. 43b. Freedom for himself and tolerance towards others in art were always one and the same thing to Schoenberg. In another place he confirms this: *Recently it has often happened that I have been asked whether certain of my compositions are "pure" twelve-tone or even twelve-tone at all. In fact—I do not know. I am always more a composer than a theoretician. And when I compose, I try to forget all theories; I only begin when I have made my mind free from all such influences. It seems to me important to warn my friends against orthodoxy. Composition with twelve tones is really only to a small degree a method which "forbids" or excludes. In the first instance it is a method which should ensure logical order and organisation; and the result of it ought to be easier comprehensibility.*

*As I have said, I cannot judge whether certain of my compositions, owing to the surprising appearance in them of consonant harmonies —surprising even to me—are to be regarded as "pure". But I am convinced that a brain which is practised in musical logic will not think of anything really false, even if it is not conscious of every-thing that it is doing.*[11]

With this premise, we can say with regard to Schoenberg's method of composition and the idea which it embodies, that it not only contradicts the purpose and the function of creating form which belong to a twelve-note series, but actually abolishes this function, if one uses more than one series in a piece—so long, at any rate, as one is not compelled to do so by a *musical* necessity, a necessity which arises intuitively from the idea of the piece and its presentation; this will then obey a law of a new kind. (What law this is would have to be searched for in actual music which has been created, and formulated accordingly). Otherwise the appearance of several series would only be of ornamental and not of organic importance; but this would mean that one was giving up the constructional values of the twelve-note series, its capacity of creating form and coherence as well as that of building chords, merely for the sake of superficial melismatic prettiness. And this without necessity; for the wonderful structure of the series contains so many possibilities of variation that a composer usually has to impose limits on himself in advance, and his sense of form has to cut out much that would complicate the music unnecessarily. Schoenberg composed a whole opera lasting several hours, "Moses and Aaron", out of a single series. On the other hand we have been able to see from the series of the Fantasy, Op. 47, what metamorphoses the series can undergo; these "mirror" the series in such an imaginative way that one seems to have two series before one. One of these consists of the first half of the actual original series as the antecedent with its own inversion a fifth lower as the consequent, and the other of the second half of the original series and its similar inversion. Creative imagination alone determines the musical "yield", and therefore the value of the series, which is its first and true conception. To ignore this "right of the first-born", with all its consequences, which must be the case when two or more series are used, would not only amount to the abolition of the law of the series and the possibilities of creating form which arise from it, but also to a contradiction of the composer's own creative imagination.

The problem which poses itself anew and has to be resolved anew with each work of art is that of achieving the greatest measure of artistic freedom and imagination within the limits of the law. The measure of perfection will depend on the measure in which this succeeds. Law, in this sense, in twelve-note music as in any other, is the ordering and unity of the musical organism of a work. The embodiment and guarantor of this law in twelve-note music is the twelve-note series, just as in the major-minor tonality it is the key and the domination of the key-note. Thus the twelve-note series represents a new form of tonality, if we understand the concept of tonality as being an ordering principle which creates coherence and form. Schoenberg describes the twelve-note series as "the first creative conception, which always occurs in the form of a thematic character". From this conception arises the series, which is then, as it were, the "mother-unit" of the whole work; for it presents the preliminary formation of the whole thematic material, of the subsidiary parts, accompanying figures and chords. It is the exclusive business of the creative faculty, the faculty which builds shapes and forms, to derive and invert these from the series. This faculty is assisted by the law of the series, which also inspires it, in that it brings together into a unity the multiplicity of shapes which are derived from the series; in this unity the basic idea of the work can express itself. This unification results from the continuous repetition of the series, of the sequence of intervals which is established in it. It permeates the whole piece like an ostinato figure from the first note to the last in all directions in the musical space, and defines what happens in this space into a whole. But it follows from this that only such a purposeful and purposive use of the twelve-note series does justice to its unifying and formative powers: that only in this way can the new tonality of twelve-note composition be realised, and that such a tonality can only arise from the use of one single series. H. H. Stuckenschmidt—to whom I express my warm thanks for his friendly interest in this work —made a serious objection to this exposition: Schoenberg's twelve-note music starts from the idea that no note should be repeated before all the other eleven have been used, for a note which is repeated too early could otherwise overweight the others, and allow the emergence of a kind of key-feeling in the sense of the major-minor tonality. But it would seem to contradict this when Schoenberg, for instance, as often happens, immediately follows the original form of the series with its retrograde in the same part. This means that, just as in the simultaneous use of two series, the eleventh, tenth, ninth notes, etc., would be repeated in the retrograde *before* the others, but clearly without endangering the purposive organisation of the music.

The analysis of this point of view finally led to a conclusion which merely reaffirmed the inner logic of Schoenberg's method. It is certainly true that the requirement that no note should be repeated before the other eleven was one of the starting-points of the method. But it was no more than that. From this point onwards Schoenberg first developed his method in various phases, always in alternation with his creative imagination, i.e. with actual composition. The predominant importance of the latter was never in doubt for him in any phase; it corrected, enlarged and altered, and one of the most important of these phases was that concerned with the concept and idea of the musical space. From this spatial perception of musical ideas it follows that one can regard and treat a series as identical with its mirror forms, as four representations of the same structure. Within such a series the twelve notes, before acquiring their own individuality, are first and above all *parts of this whole*, i.e. of the series, fixed in position through the melodic (i.e. interval-) relationship of each note with that which precedes and follows it— a relationship which always remains unaltered. This relationship with one another—hence the "Method of composition with twelve notes related only to one another"—restores to the notes an affinity with one another which is so strong that even an earlier repetition of a note (as in the connection between original and retrograde in the query mentioned above) does not remove it from its coherence *in the series*, but allows it to be sensed first and above all as part of the series; i.e. the series, as a complete structure, is repeated (in a retrograde manner), not the individual note. And now Schoenberg's formulation acquires its deeper meaning, when he says that *"within the series"* no note should be repeated before the rest. Only a repetition outside the sequence of the series, as is the case with the appearance of a second series which is quite differently arranged melodically, removes the original connection of the note with the series, and thereby also removes its function of creating coherence.

In any case, Schoenberg considerably removed the force of this objection in practice—this is now clear—with his endeavour so to arrange the first half of the series that its inversion a fifth lower contains the notes of the second half (even if in a different order) as an accompaniment, and vice versa. Through this the original series is heard complete in the vertical dimension before the retrograde form starts; then the latter contains no untimely repetition of the notes.

14. *Typology of the series—questions of notation* We have deliberately omitted to give a typology of the series [i.e. a systematic account of the different possible types of series] which goes beyond anything said in this chapter. In any case it is clearly superfluous in respect of Schoenberg and his music, as with him the melodic law of the series always arises from the basic conception of the piece. Any other indication of the principle according to which the intervals of the series should follow one another, an indication which is musically convincing and which is to be regarded as applicable in all cases, can nowhere be definitely discovered—up to now, that is—from the music that has been actually written!—and could only restrict the free breath of the creative process.

The question of notation was treated by Schoenberg purely from a practical point of view, that of the easiest method of reading the notes and of the most practical notation from the point of view of the performer's technique. As the principle of enharmonic change in our well-tempered system also applies to twelve-note music, this is the suggestion that we shall give here too.

CHAPTER VII

INVENTION AND VARIATION OF TWELVE-NOTE SERIES—THE
FUNCTION OF RHYTHM

*I. Melodic variations—the isorhythmic principle*
*II. The creation and function of harmony in twelve-*
*note music*

THE composer who wishes to concern himself practically with
twelve-note composition should now thoroughly work through
the contents of the chapter on the twelve-note series; for, in
Schoenberg's words, the series is the "preliminary formation
of the entire thematic material" of a piece. In order to invent and
derive this material from it, one must have a complete grasp of
the structure and function of the series. One must, as it were,
trace it with one's musical senses, and really "get the feeling"
of it in the true meaning of the phrase; one must make the series
and its mirror forms completely "one's own". One must know
how to use it in a linear manner as a whole or in its groups; one
must know the possibilities and variations of melodic tension
which are contained in it; one must know its interval-
correspondences, both within the series itself, and between the
series and its mirror-forms; one must know the relations of the
different forms of the series to one another—which may show,
for instance, that the series can be more closely related to its
inversion than to its retrograde form, or vice versa; this will
depend on the structure of the series, for instance if its note-groups
contain symmetrical arrangements of notes.

We would next recommend the study of this whole subject by
means of the examples of series from Schoenberg's works; these
can be found in the tables of musical illustrations in this book.
They are structures which stem from the imagination and creative

hand of a master, and therefore certainly contain everything of musically constructive value which one could demand from a series of the kind. A composer should only take his first steps in a path which is good and well tried-out—a model one, in fact; for it is clear that the series is the starting-point for everything else, and is the real key to the music of whatever work is under discussion. It must meet all the demands of the imagination, and of both conscious and unconscious construction. If the series, being the foundation of the musical building, is not "right", then more and more difficulties will arise in the course of the composition. It is generally easier—in principle, at any rate—to make the series "right" by the unconscious and immediate means of the primary musical conception of a work, rather than by constructing it consciously; and the former is also a more reliable way of attaining the musical results—for the latter presupposes great experience and maturity in composition and the power of thinking logically in music. Therefore the young musician would do better first of all to rely on his own gifts and powers of imagination.

When he has assimilated the properties of Schoenberg's series, and the musical ideas which are at the bottom of them—that is to say, the "basic shapes", together with the individual features of the musical material, the principle which controls its ordering, and the germinating forces which are provided thereby—he should attempt as his next step to invent thematic ideas himself and derive the series from these. The more his musical train of thought is of a non-tonal kind, the easier this will be for him. And it is only on this premise that there is really any purpose in his attempting to compose in this manner; and then only if the composer endeavours and succeeds in mastering his material and his imagination, instead of being mastered by them. Otherwise, if there is no inner musical necessity, the result will only be a quite superficially "modern" work of doubtful value.

It is best to begin with six-note ideas, in the manner of a thematic antecedent, and to form the six-note series and its mirror forms from this. This should be done systematically, with all kinds of musical ideas; first in one part, then in two, either with a main theme and its accompaniment (with the accompaniment sometimes in chords, sometimes in figurations), or contrapuntally.

In the tables of musical illustrations, examples of the most varied kinds will be found, to fit all such cases. We should specially mention the Fantasy, Op. 47, as its series—as already stated—appears in two six-note forms.

In making these attempts at composition only one form of the series, the original, should be used at first; then its mirror forms can be introduced later. We recommend that, following the tendency shown by Schoenberg, the inversion—whether it is a fifth lower or at some other transposition—should consist of the remaining six notes. This will not succeed immediately and completely—nor, if it does not, is it necessarily unusable.

The next task is to find the thematic consequent from the remaining six notes, but in a different order—unless this has arisen immediately as a musical idea. This is again primarily a task of musical composition, not of mathematical calculation; it is a question of following one's own powers of musical imagination.

The third phase will then consist of the invention of twelve-note themes. This will cause fewer difficulties if the composer has already intensively grasped the musical conceptions given shape by Schoenberg, if he has worked with them practically and grasped their musical consequences; then the series will appear of itself, like a ripe fruit. If it is not a complete series, then one must try carefully to "correct" it according to the *musical* purpose desired, i.e. so that the musical character of the basic conception is not altered thereby, and in favourable circumstances may even gain perspective.

In some circumstances—this is a question of practical experiment—perhaps another method will prove to be easier to follow and more instructive; as a preparation for the invention of one's own six-note and twelve-note musical ideas, one can invent thematic shapes from half or whole series taken from Schoenberg's works. This will give practice in inventing thematic material out of a given series, and can be regarded as a parallel to the composition of variations on an extraneous theme.

Before we continue to discuss the invention of thematic material from a series, we must first deal in detail with the possibilities of melodic and harmonic variation of a series, the knowledge of which is indispensable for the use of a series in composition, and also with the function of rhythm. On this point we should say with all possible emphasis, that the observations which we make in the following pages are derived individually from Schoenberg's works, and merely serve to give a clear and systematic survey of the methods of procedure in composition which were invented and practised by Schoenberg. They should in no way be regarded as *recipes* which show "how it is done" (which has nothing to do with art), even where such an impression might be created, nor as *rules* which have to be followed unconditionally. The purpose of these observations, apart from that mentioned already, is quite different; it is to show how inexhaustible is the imagination of a master in "inventing out of a law", and how the very strictness of this law can stimulate the imagination and become an impulse to creation; and how music gains strength from the imaginative interpretation of a law. Thus the meaning of the law is purely compositional and should only be understood as such.

## I. *Melodic Variations of a Series*

The necessity of varying the melodic sequence of the notes of a series in its use in composition generally arises from the limitless freedom of invention which a work of art demands; and especially from the fact that a certain danger of monotony resides (from the nature of things) in the continuous repetition of the series. For the purpose of a practical survey we will here sum up the possibilities of melodic variation of a series which have already been dealt with in another connection, and will give further details about some new ones.

Melodic alterations can arise through:

1. *Transposition of a note into the higher or lower octaves*

(a) This expands or contracts the tension between the intervals at a particular place in the series (or motif, theme or chord) by one or more octaves.

(b) The complementary interval arises. Both kinds of melodic variation have already been discussed. Compare Tables VI and IX, bars 1–16 from the first movement of the fourth String Quartet, with bars 165–169; and Table V K from the Wind Quintet, Op. 26.

2. *Use of the mirror forms and transpositions of a series* The alternative use of one of the mirror forms in the same theme (or figure or melody) produces a rich method of melodic variation which is often very far-reaching. Schoenberg uses it both (a) for variation in the repetition of an idea in the course of a movement, and also (b) for variation in the repetition of the sections of a thematic form (e.g. first and third sections of a three-section song form).

(a) The following example shows the main theme of the third movement of the fourth String Quartet, Op. 37; it is recitative-like, and is played in unison:

It is derived from the original form of the series, transposed a whole tone lower. However its reprise uses the inversion at a fifth lower of the transposed series. Page 83 gives the first of the three sections of the main theme of the first movement of the same work, bars 1–5; in table VIII E, bars 95–98, this is repeated in a shortened form derived from the inversion.

(b) The consequent of the theme of the Variations in the Serenade, Op. 24 (see p. 62)—a theme which is written in period form—is the varied repetition of the antecedent; it uses the retrograde series, which produces very considerable *melodic* variation, but the rhythm and phrasing remain the same. The sixteen-bar main theme of the first movement of the fourth String Quartet (Table VI A) is in three sections. The first section, bars 1–5, is repeated in bars 10 (with up-beat)–14, here using the retrograde form of the series, with the rhythm remaining the same.

In order to be able to recognise the repetition of the particular thematic shape or melody, in spite of such considerable melodic variation as is effected, in particular, by the use of the retrograde and retrograde inversion, we find that in these cases the *isorhythmic principle* is used, i.e. the rhythm of the thematic shape is repeated exactly in all essentials, and also its phrasing. This balances the free *melodic* development and indeed makes it possible; for it ensures the musical coherence and the identity of the thematic shape on its repetition. But naturally it is essential that the rhythm should be very characteristic and marked.

The examples in Table V K are taken from Schoenberg *(Style and Idea)* and show numerous isorhythmic variants of the Rondo theme from the Wind Quintet, Op. 26, arrived at through use of the retrograde form and by exchanging the positions of its two halves.

Which transpositions of the four forms of the series, and how many of them—eleven of each form are possible—are to be used in a piece, depends on:

(a) The kind and the length of the piece; whether it is to be an orchestral or a chamber music work, an opera or a song;

(b) The structure and the subdivisions of the series. We have already discussed this in connection with symmetrical series. A reduction of the four forms to two or so limits the musical capacity of the series and therefore the length of the piece; or in certain circumstances it may increase the number of transpositions used;

(c) The melodic (i.e. intervallic) relationships between the forms of the series and their transpositions. We have also already discussed the musical consequences of relationships which arise from the presence of the same interval in the various forms and transpositions, and also the musical connection between a series and its inversion a fifth lower. Schoenberg also transfers this relationship to the transpositions, combining a transposed series with its inversion a fifth lower. Thus the third movement of the fourth String Quartet begins with the original series transposed to start on C; the reprise in bar 664 begins with its inversion a fifth lower, starting on F. But the original series transposed on to C is again the inversion a fifth lower of the inversion starting on G, which itself arose from the original series starting on D (first movement, bar 1 ff.); so that the first notes of the series here form a kind of circle of fifths (Table XII Q and XIV T).

But there are still more subtle melodic connections which remove the need for a special "choice" of the transposition to be used, as they arise unforcedly from the course of the music itself, like modulations in tonal music. Here are two characteristic examples of this from the fourth Quartet:

The original series which starts in bar 650 on F in the first violin, has already been prepared three bars earlier by the notes F—E—C, also in the first violin, and again by the last crotchet of bar 649 in the second violin: E—F → F—E—C—D flat (Table XIII S).

The step of a minor second with which the original series of the work begins, and which comes in it five times altogether, not only creates motivic connections between the series (e.g. O 1—2—3 = RI 10—9—8; I 1—2—3 = R 10—9—8; O 8—9—10 = R 3—2—1 etc.), which we will discuss in further detail in a later section (p. 120ff.), but also acts as a starting-point for transpositions. E.g. the original series begins with D—C sharp; one inversion begins with C sharp—D, and the original series a fifth higher which goes with this inversion starts with G sharp—G (see bars 638 f.). But this G sharp (A flat)—G is already contained in the main theme as the 9th and 10th notes of the original series.

In general it is Schoenberg's intention that transpositions which lie further afield—as well as occasional liberties and deviations from the normal order of the notes—should preferably appear in the later sections of a piece, by which time the ear has got accustomed to the series.

3. *Distribution of a series between the horizontal and vertical dimensions*   The melodic variations discussed in Sections 1 and 2 above leave the melodic structure of the series itself unaltered, and always present the latter in a twelve-note horizontal form. Another kind of melodic variation arises from the concept of the unity of musical space, and rests on the principle, already stated on p. 82, of the coherence between harmonic and melodic phenomena. This allows one to take individual notes or groups of notes (see Section 4 below) out of the melodic line and to sound them simultaneously with the latter in the form of a chord, an accompanying figure or a subsidiary part. Thus here too the main part is predominant, and determines not only the musical development, but, from this, the treatment of the series also. It has complete melodic freedom, without thereby denying the law of the series. Schoenberg even gives this "breaking up" of the melodic sequence a motivic purpose of its own by means of a certain regularity in the horizontal and vertical distribution of the notes. The notes which are important thematically, as well as the accompanying notes, are combined into groups; or, to put it another way, the subdivision of the series into groups furthers a regularity of this kind. *The distribution* (of the notes) *may*

*be varied or developed according to circumstances, in a manner comparable to the changes of what I call the "Motive of the Accompaniment."*[2] This goes together with the varying groupings of the twelve notes.

The two-dimensional treatment of the series can:

1.  Vary a thematic or melodic formation on its repetition in the manner of the "abbreviation" which occurs in classical music, by leaving out individual notes or groups of notes (i.e. phrases). See Table X L, bars 239–244, compared with Table VI A bars 1–6.

2.  Join separate notes together in motifs or phrases which are recognised as such from the course of the music; or the notes of these motifs and phrases may have originally been present as a melodic group within the series (Table X K bar 226; Table XI N bar 434, first violin; Table XIV U bar 746).

3.  Cause the appearance of new melodic and thematic shapes (Table IV H bars 1–8; Table XI N bars 433–435; Table IX I bars 188 ff.—second violin and viola, and first violin and 'cello. Note here the development of a subsidiary part in the second violin out of the motif of the minor second. Table XIV U bars 747–749; Table XIII S bar 655: both violin parts are based on the inversion, and the accompanying second violin plays a variant of the first violin part—notes 1—2—3 as opposed to 1—2—4).

The notes, intervals or note-groups which have been taken out of the series in this way (see Section 4) can:

(a) Be held on like a pedal-point (Table XIV U bar 740 ff.).

(b) Form chords (Table X K bars 224–5; XI N 433–7).

(c) Appear in figures (Table XI N bars 438–9), or

(d) In contrapuntal or subsidiary parts (Table XII R, bars 630–1; XIV U bars 747–9).

If two or more of the four forms of the series are used simultaneously, (a) the notes, (b) the intervals or (c) the note-groups which they have in common can serve to link these series together; by treating these elements separately as new combinations of notes, the remaining notes of each series can thus acquire a new melodic sequence.

(a) Table V I, bars 114–117, Coda. The note E flat in the flute is the first note of the original series; the B in the clarinet is the fourth note of the original series and the second note of the inversion. Table XIV U bars 740–749 is especially instructive: in bar 745 the viola has the eighth note of the retrograde inversion, which is also the third note of the retrograde. The 'cello has the twelfth note of the RI (= fourth of R) and the first of R (= first of O in bar 746). Table IX H, bars 175–8, show several connections of series. The last quaver of bar 176 is especially interesting; the B flat in the 'cello is the fifth note of RI and also the seventh of R in the second violin. Also in bar 175 the first violin has F as the final note in the main part; the I-series of this has already ended with the E, while the F is taken from the O series in the viola. The whole of this is a counterpart to bar 169, whereby this repetition acquires a motivic character! In bar 169 the first violin plays the first note of the O series, which then goes over into the second violin part. The up-beat A flat before bar 178 in the first violin is the last note of the R series in the viola and also the beginning of the O series. Musically the main part here is linked to the rhythm of bar 177.

(b) The missing last two notes of the RI in the 'cello in bar 177, D and C sharp, appear in the following bar, but rearranged as C sharp—D and thus at once form the beginning of the I which follows. Table IV F bar 193: the interval of a seventh between E in the bassoon and D in the clarinet is here a "pivot-interval" between O and I. The same may be seen in IV G bar 360 (clarinet).

(c) Table IV G bar 361: notes 2—3—4 of O and 4—3—2 of I (clarinet) are common. Table IX H bars 169–174: the first violin has notes 1 and 6 of O, the second violin has 2—3—4—5; see also the second violin and viola parts. Table XII R bars 636–7 are derived from O and RI respectively. The first group of O, the notes C—B—G, is identical with notes 10—9—8 of RI. These three notes are played by the viola as an ostinato accompanying figure in both bars, while the remaining notes and note-groups appear in the other instruments.

Apart from the details given above regarding the series, these examples contain, from the musical point of view, a mass of subtleties in the motivic development and in the fluid presentation of the ideas, in the clear division into main and subsidiary parts by means of the quicker or slower development of these parts, and in the musical coherence between the main part and the accompaniment. We recommend a special study of these points as the necessary supplement to the study of the series and as the real musical purpose of serial composition.

4. *Exchange of note-groups within a series*   We have already referred to the formal function of the subdivision of a series into groups. This has the effect of:

(a) A definite ordering, when the main part and the accompaniment or subsidiary parts are formed from a single series.

(b) A "loosening-up" of the series, in the sense of a more elastic treatment of it in both the vertical and horizontal dimensions.

(c) These note-groups can be regarded and treated as small independent series. This allows them to change places with one another, especially when they possess an interval which is common to two or more groups, and thus provides a motivic relationship. Changing places means:

(i) Altering the sequence of the groups as wholes, or

(ii) Allowing them to overlap one another, or

(iii) The combination of both possibilities.

The possibility of treating the note-groups in this way resembles a "setting of them in space"—an idea that can be clearly grasped from the conception of the Musical Space discussed above. The melodic variation which arises from this is almost unlimited, and, as well as variations in the normal sense, it creates new melodic formations of many kinds, which are indirectly derived from the series.

Without claiming to have included everything which Schoenberg's inexhaustible musical imagination created from possibilities of this kind, let us now try to discuss some fundamental methods of procedure in composition which arise from the subdivision of a series into groups.

In connection with the division of a series into groups, possibilities of melodic variation arise through:

(a) *Changing the relative positions of the groups*  Table VI B[1] shows the beginning of the Gavotte from the Suite, Op. 25.

The beginning of the first movement of Op. 26 (Table III A) changes round the four groups of three notes in the original series in such a way that the theme uses groups 2 and 4 and the accompaniment 1 and 3, in the order 3—1—4—2. The groups enter quite separately, but overlap one another. The symmetry between the two halves of the series also favours the musical co-ordination between theme and accompaniment; the accompaniment contains the intervals which are characteristic of the theme (leap of a sixth downwards—step of a second upwards) without any rhythm, and combines them in chords. Note the variation in the accompaniment which begins on the last crotchet of bar 3. The strengthening of the musical coherence between theme and accompaniment is very clearly shown in this example.

(b) *Overlapping of the groups in their normal or altered sequence* The theme of the Scherzo of Op. 26 (Table III D) is also invented from the original series. It is a very instructive parallel to the main theme of the first movement; although the character of the accompaniment is quite different, the use of the same series has the effect of creating a close relationship with the first movement, both harmonically and melodically. The original series is used twice simultaneously: in the accompaniment it has the normal order of note-groups 1—2—3—4, but in the theme the order is 2—3—4—1, simultaneously effacing the division between the groups.

The Reprise of the main theme (bars 1–15) in the second movement of Op. 26 (see Table IV E) is anticipated by the bassoon in bar 61 in canonic imitation, using the second half of the original series. Notice the melodic variation, when the fourth note-group is followed a bar later by the second note-group with the same theme. There is continuous overlapping of the groups, also an exchange of the sequence of the notes within the groups, but only in the accompaniment. The leap of a sixth, which is characteristic of the theme, also appears as a motif in the accompaniment (oboe bar 65, horn bars 66 and 67, oboe bar 67) and naturally takes precedence over the series; the latter is handled in such a way that the motif can appear anywhere where the music demands it.

(c) *Splitting up of the groups*  Just as, by splitting up a series, its notes can serve as musical material in the horizontal and vertical dimensions simultaneously, so a similar procedure, with similar effect as regards melodic variation, can be carried out with the note-group.

The Minuet from Op. 25 (Table VI A[1]) begins with the second note-group, which itself at once splits into two parts. The upper part begins with notes 5 and 7, the lower part, with its characteristic rhythm, has notes 6 and 8.

In bar 655 of the fourth Quartet (Table XIII S) the two violins on the one hand and the viola and 'cello on the other each derive their parts from one series split up into groups. Bar 746 (Table XIV U) shows three parts formed from three groups belonging to a series.

(d) *New groupings*  There are two examples of this in Op. 26 (Table III C). In the Coda of the first movement, bars 209–212, there are three groups of four notes, arranged, 1—12—6—7, 2—3—4—5, 8—9—10—11. There is a parallel to this in the second movement, bars 196 ff. (Table IV F); four three-note groups, through having appeared as chords, produce three four-note lines and a four-note phrase (horn bars 191–195, bassoon bar 196 ff.).

(e) *Exchange of identical groups between two or more series*  If two or more forms of the series appear at the same time, then they too can exchange their groups with one another.

There is a good example of this in the fourth Quartet. In bar 645 (Table XIII S), in the demisemiquaver figure in the first violin the last group of the retrograde 3—2—1 is played as 1—2—3; the same thing happens in bars 647 and 648 to the last groups of the retrograde and the inversion respectively. Thus this is no arbitrary or isolated variation but has a motivic significance. Note further the musical variety of the corresponding arrangement of the groups in the other instruments. In bar 645 in the viola the group C sharp—D—F sharp from the retrograde (motif a) is identical with the beginning of the inversion in the first violin (bar 646, motif a¹). Thus the main part which starts here has already been prepared melodically in the previous bar— a parallel to similar harmonic turns in tonal music. Similarly in bar 647 the first violin, with the notes F—E—C—(C sharp) as a mirror form (1—2—3) of the last group of the retrograde (3—2—1), prepares the new transposition of the original series, F—E—C—C sharp which begins in bar 650. See also bar 649, last crotchet in the second violin, which is a mirror form of the last group of the retrograde and has a similar effect.

Naturally, identical groups can also be found in two series without mirror forms. Table XII R, bars 636 and 637: in both bars the viola has an ostinato figure C—B—G, which is both 1—2—3 of O and 10—9—8 of RI. Also Table XIV S; bars 660—661: the viola has G flat—F—D flat, which is first 1—2—3 of O and then 10—9—8 of RI. This is introduced in bar 659 by changing over the last two notes of R, G flat—F instead of F—G flat; again a variation of the series for musical reasons!

(f) *Variation in the repetition of note-groups*  Here are three interesting examples of this: Table XIII S, bar 651. On the last semiquaver of the bar the 'cello repeats the last group of the RI, which had already appeared in the preceding chord, and thereby links itself to the lowest note of the chord, C sharp: the sequence is C sharp—C—E—F. In the following bar 652 the first violin takes over this C sharp—C, (which now continues differently, with G sharp—A) this is the beginning of a transposition of the original series. Thus transpositions arise out of the musical—i.e. melodic —development. The demisemiquaver figure in the 'cello in bar 651 also has a motivic character in the following bars (second violin, viola and 'cello parts).

Table XIII S, bar 653: on the last crotchet the second violin repeats in a shortened form the phrase of the first violin, 4—3—2. Note how in bar 654 the first violin takes up the G—F sharp again ("link-technique"); it now leads to a change of the order of the notes within the RI group.

Table VIII G: finally, the transitional passage which leads to the reprise of the main theme in bar 165 of the first movement of the fourth String Quartet contains a new and very original kind of repetition of note-groups. Bar 157, with preliminary up-beat, shows the entry of the 'cello with a motif which begins with the first three-note group of R, and goes eight times through all the four instruments in imitation; each time it begins with the same group of three quavers, C—G—A flat, but each time these are followed by a different note from the remaining ones which make up the retrograde.

## II. *The creation and function of harmony in twelve-note music*

Before we enquire into the variations in harmony which are possible in chords derived from the series, we must discuss these chords themselves, and the kinds of harmonic organisation which exist in twelve-note music. What harmonies can arise? How do they arise? What are their functions?

The first question can be answered quite shortly. All chords consisting of from three to twelve notes can appear, and with all thinkable combinations of the twelve notes of our well-tempered system. Thus triads of tonal structure can appear too, as, for instance, the "Ode to Napoleon" shows. But these, like *all* chord-structures in twelve-note music, are of purely local importance and do not produce harmonic *progressions* which have the effect of creating form, as happens in tonal music; for the relationship to the key-note is missing. This is the decisive and fundamental difference between twelve-note music and the harmonic procedures in tonal music. This also answers the question of the function of harmonic formations and chord sequences in twelve-note music; in this music a chord has only a function as a sound or a rhythm (or a motif) in the sense of giving a harmonic accent. This either (a) helps the subdivision of a small musical space, for instance, by accentuating a melodic centre of gravity; or (b) it serves to enhance the musical characteristics of its immediate surroundings which are organically connected with it. As already stated, the same applies to a sequence of several chords.

The local organic connection of chords or chord-sequences with the musical events in general arises directly from the way in which the chords themselves are produced; they are formed out of the series, following the principle that the latter allows of emanation in both the horizontal (melodic), and in the vertical (harmonic) dimensions. As we have already seen, this principle serves to co-ordinate the melodic and harmonic elements, and thus assists the unification of the musical purpose of a piece. Regarded in this way, one can thus speak of the formal effect of the formation of chords in twelve-note music, even if this is differently ordered from that in tonal music. This chord-formation never occurs arbitrarily, but always organically, according to the formative function of the law of the series. The composer's powers of imagination decide how this law is to be handled and varied in different cases.

Chords can arise out of the series either indirectly, as the result of contrapuntal or other similar part-writing, or directly out of the series itself.

1. *Chord-formation through part-writing*   Compostion with twelve-notes is primarily and predominantly of a contrapuntal nature, as has been shown both in practice and in the rules and indications derived from practice—but this by no means prevents it from being used harmonically also. It also corresponds to polyphonic music in that in both cases the chord-like sounds which arise from part-writing have no "obligation" in the sense of harmonic function. This applies both to each combination of simultaneous sounds regarded separately (one need only think of the similar formations which occur in J. S. Bach's motets, for instance), and also to their combination in chord-sequences, which—at the time when the music of the Netherlands school, which was based on the medieval modes, was in full flower—did not show a harmonic sense which corresponded to the laws

of tonality. The combinations of sounds which arise out of linear part-writing are "correct" in spite of all their lack of "obligation", both in polyphonic and in twelve-note music, as they are justified by the melodic logic of the individual parts and by the ear of the composer (whose share in our demonstrations is not always specifically mentioned, but must naturally always be borne in mind).

2. *Direct formation of chords from the series and its mirror forms* All chords in twelve-note music which do not arise through part-writing are obtained directly out of the series and its mirror forms or transpositions; the melodic sequence of intervals in the series can also be combined harmonically to make a simultaneous sound.

Clearly chords derived from transposed series have the same structure as those derived from the original series and its mirror forms; for, as with key-transpositions in tonal music, the intervals and the sequence of intervals in the transposed series are the same and produce the same harmonies as those in the original series.

As against this, the four forms of the series themselves show two different aspects in the vertical dimension. The following section of a series shows that the corresponding chordal combinations (a) in the O and R series on the one hand, and (b) in the I and RI series on the other, produce different chords.

However, their relationship is obvious, and is due to the structural similarity of the four forms of the series. It approximately corresponds to the relationship between these two chords in tonal music:

The variations in harmony which are possible in twelve-note music thus arise through one of the following causes:

(a) Change in octave pitch of one or more notes in a chord; the variation which arises in this way can be compared with the inversions of a tonal chord. One or more notes in the chord can change their octave pitch, and the number of possible variations clearly increases with the number of notes in the chord.

One example to represent many is shown in Table VI A, last crotchet of bar 7 of the fourth Quartet; first violin, viola and 'cello play the same chord as on the first two crotchets, but in a varied arrangement. The type of harmonic variation which corresponds to this can be found in contrapuntal writing, when the parts exchange places in double or multiple counterpoint (Table XI M, bars 415 ff.).

(b) Exchange of place between the note-groups in a series. Examples of both (a) and (b) can be found in the second movement of Op. 26, Table IV F. Compare bars 191–2 with 196–7. The three-note groups of the original series change places, and at the same time the pitch of the notes within each group is altered.

(c) Exchanging of complementary groups between the main part and the accompaniment. See Table VI A: the first six bars present the complete O series in the first violin as the main part. It is accompanied by three-part chords which, together with the section of the main part which is played simultaneously with them, complete the O series, so that this appears once horizontally in the main part and also four times vertically in the accompaniment at the same time, made up out of the complementary groups of three notes. In spite of complete regularity in the sequence of the groups, this provides variation in the *sequence* of the chords and also varied arrangements of the same chord. See also bars 10–16. Bars 7–9 are derived from the I series in the same way.

A comparison with bars 243–4 (Table X L) shows another kind of variation of harmony (and sonority) built out of the same O series.

(d) Coupling of two or more forms of the series. Table XIII S, bar 655 is based on the O series and its inversion a fifth lower; bars 656–7 on the R series and its inversion a fifth lower. In bar 655 the second violin plays the "remains" of the I series which is the main part in the first violin, and connects this in chords with the O series in the viola and 'cello.

The appearance of tonal chord-formations in twelve-note music calls for a short discussion. We spoke elsewhere of the effect of coming to a conclusion in music, as opposed to the music just stopping, and recognised this to be a criterion of the quality of the music. This effect of concluding does not only depend on the final harmonic progression V-I, but will be prepared by a good composer well in advance, in the so-called final section or Coda. In contrast to these classical methods of procedure, many compositions which are either non-tonal or have no pronounced tonality simply end with a major or minor triad the first appearance of which is also its last. The pleasant, satisfying effect given by such a chord—though it is musically completely "hanging in the air"—is not the result of a logical development towards a conclusion, a harmonic (and at the same time a general) development which tends towards the tonic; it merely depends on the entirely primitive and momentary effect of "solution" provided by a harmonic *deus ex machina*, and on the association with the customary "cliché" effect of a tonal final chord—but it has no basis in a musical procedure. So a chord of this sort merely remains an ornamental, "pretty" flourish, arbitrarily inserted; it could have been put in just as well (or badly) a few bars earlier or later with the same recipe-like effect.

Such arbitrariness is alien to a good composer, and especially to a master like Schoenberg. In this connection let us look at the triad E flat—G—B flat which concludes the "Ode to Napoleon". The series which is the basis of this work (Table XV B[1]) is so built that it shows a tonal tendency, both melodically and harmonically, without, however, giving way to this tendency. This is sufficient as an organic precondition to justify and explain the appearance of triads with a tonal structure. Analysis clearly shows that among these tonal triads the chord E flat—G—B flat becomes increasingly preponderant. A cursory glance through the score shows the following correspondences in this connection; in bar 64 of the piece (which is 267 bars long altogether) the first violin, at the words "voice of victory" has the well-known quotation from Beethoven's Fifth Symphony, which also explains the later domination of this (quasi) E flat chord—the relative major key to C minor. Further on, this triad can be found as a chord, for instance, on the second crotchet of bar 95, and from there on it appears more and more frequently towards the end; in bars 221-2 it appears melodically and harmonically, also in bars 242-4 and 252—so that the quasi-dominant-tonic chords of the last two bars, on B flat and E flat, are natural and right as the product of an organic development from the first conception of the work and from its note-series. In this work Schoenberg shows some surprising inner connections between tonal and twelve-note music, and a way of combining them organically which shows them to be two different sides of the same process of human thought and creation.

*The function of rhythm in twelve-note music*   Rhythm has a special formal function in Schoenberg's twelve-note music, in addition to its motivic function and to that of creating subdivisions; these latter functions have remained unaltered from what they were in the classical tradition. The new function is connected with the isorhythmic principle mentioned above (p. 117). To put it in a few words, one can say that rhythm can appear as (a) an independent rhythmical motif or shape, (b) as an element in a musical motif, as a motivic rhythm (see p. 136), and (c) as a means of phrasing, i.e. it determines the different subdivisions in the course of a melody and in this—a tendency of modern music in general—it particularly prevents too great emphasis on the strong beats of the bar, which often resists a phrasing which would correspond more fully to the musical purpose in question. This goes together with the increasing use of thematic and melodic formations of uneven bar-lengths in the music of the last hundred years, and with the tendency to avoid symmetrical subdivisions.* The functions of rhythm mentioned above will naturally often be fused with one another or supplement one another. Their increased share in the shaping of music, in the characteristic "intonation" and in the perspective given to the thematic ideas, is obvious in the music of our time in general, and in twelve-note music in particular.

*Connection of the repetitions of series—choice of the sequence of series* Which forms or transpositions of the series should follow the preceding ones will be determined by the internal and external ear of the composer and by the needs of the musical construction. At first there will be some difficulty in connecting the repetitions of the series with one another without joins, and in letting them lead on from one to another in such a way that the flow of the music does not suffer. Fluid presentation of the musical ideas is one of the most important criteria of good composition. The close connection which exists between the choice of the sequence of series and the connection of two series with one another is obvious; indeed the one conditions and influences the other.

The three chief means of joining two series together in a linear manner are the note, the motif and the chord.

We already know the *note* as a means of connection from the "link-technique" of classical music; for example, when the consequent of a theme begins with the last note of the antecedent and continues the former in a fluent manner. Two series can be connected together in a similar way.

The *motif* can join two series together if it links the last note

---

* A systematic attempt to formulate these tendencies is the basis of Boris Blacher's method of composition with "variable metres".

or notes of one series to the first note or notes of the next one. This, too, is an imitation of a classical model, in cases where, for instance, two phrases or sections of themes are joined together by a subsidiary part which goes across the join.

The *chord* can make a convincing connection between two series, especially when these contain the same chords as one another, either partly—e.g. in certain note-groups—or as wholes. The latter is the case (see p. 128) with an original series and its retrograde, or with an inversion and its corresponding retrograde inversion. Series with a special structure, especially symmetrical ones as in the "Ode to Napoleon", can also produce other connections by means of chords which are identical in different forms of the series.

The connecting effect of such chords depends on their dual meaning; two series of this kind have the same intervals as each other and are only differentiated by their different melodic (i.e. horizontal) sequence. But since this cannot be recognised in a chordal contraction, the chord can belong to either of the two series.

In all the three cases above it is primarily musical influences which determine the choice of the sequence of the series in the linear dimension. To this also belongs the practice which has already been mentioned and was increasingly favoured by Schoenberg, that of using series whose inversion or retrograde inversion starts a perfect fifth lower than the original or retrograde series. This applies not only to the linear use of one series after another, but also and especially to their simultaneous use, to the coupling of two forms of the series in parallel. A survey of the first fifty out of the ninety bars which make up the Largo movement of the fourth Quartet shows an almost equal use of the four forms of the series; the O and RI each appear fifteen times, the I fourteen and the R thirteen. Here all the series are transposed,* and there are seven different transpositions each of the O and RI series, and six each of the I and R. But wherever two series are

* Transposed series are not specially marked as such in the tables of musical examples, as it is easy to see the transposition by the first note of the series in relation to that of the original form of the series.

coupled in parallel in these fifty bars, the two series, without exception, appear at the interval of a fifth to one another, as has been mentioned above. This seems to show the presence of a principle, or at any rate a method of procedure, which uses the natural acoustical relations of notes for the additional strengthening of the musical material.

## CHAPTER VIII

# THE INVENTION OF THEMATIC MATERIAL FROM A TWELVE-NOTE SERIES

*The motivic character of the twelve-note series and the consequences of this for the technique of composition—The "motivic interval" and "motivic rhythm" as independent elements of a musical motif—The invention of various kinds of motivic material, shown in the Fourth String Quartet, Op. 37, the Ode to Napoleon, Op. 41, the Fantasy for Violin and Piano, Op. 47 and the Three Songs, Op. 48.*

THE last two chapters were concerned with the twelve-note series and its treatment in the technique of composition, as shown in Schoenberg's works. In this an attempt was made to present the subject in a precise and at the same time undogmatic manner, contrasting the law of the series with the freedom of its interpretation, and showing this by musical examples. Though the emphasis was on the actual technique, it was almost always derived from or demonstrated by the musical substance of Schoenberg's compositions; for without connection and interplay with the musical substance we would soon be moving in a space devoid of music, and all discussions and formulations would remain artistically fruitless. The change of emphasis to the practical side necessarily follows when we concern ourselves, in the following pages, with the invention of thematic material out of the series.

Inventing themes is identical with giving them shape. Here it means shaping them out of the series, which arises out of the basic conception of the piece as the preliminary formation of the entire thematic material. This shaping takes place through the use of the artistic means which still apply here—those which were used and developed by classical and pre-classical music on the basis of the principle of repetition, and the principle of motivic working in polyphonic music, or motivic variation in homophonic music. Thus the circle of our discussions begins to close, as these are leading us back to the point from which we started, the analysis of Beethoven's Op. 10, No. 1. This analysis, originating from and guided by the idea of Schoenberg's composition with twelve notes (which ensures the unity and form of a work), proved the correctness and general applicability of this very idea in a *classical* manner and by a classical example. This analysis touched on both the question of the musical substance, out of which the themes are invented and shaped, and also on this process of invention itself, from the point of view of classical music.

We saw how everything in the work was implicitly contained in the four-bar basic shape of the first movement, the first creative conception; and how the thematic material of the whole sonata was invented out of this basic shape by means of repetition and variation of both its melodic and rhythmical content. As this content (because it is characteristic of the basic shape) is repeated frequently during the course of the piece in many different shapes, it is *motivic* in form and character. The definition of the basic shape, as the "firm connection together of one or more motifs and their more or less varied repetitions", corresponds to this, as does that of the musical motif, as the smallest unit of form, consisting of at least one interval and one rhythm.

The melodic and rhythmical elements in the motif, however, each possess a motivic character of their own, as both are used independently of each other in the course of the piece, exactly or in varied forms. This independence makes it possible to have new combinations of the motivic intervals and motivic rhythms of the basic shape, which are shaped in correspondence to the thematic function, i.e. as a subsidiary, transitional, concluding idea, etc., and produce all the remaining thematic material which is necessary for this. All these characteristics of the presentation, shaping and development of musical ideas out of the motivic substance apply both to tonal and to twelve-note music.

Only one difference remains: in tonal music the motivic interval is derived from the key (scale, or triad), in twelve-note music from the series. This does not in the least affect the fundamental continuity of the process of composition sketched above, as it has been built up in the last 300 years; rather it augments and enlarges this process by means of a new kind of treatment of the motivic material. For Schoenberg has drawn consequences from the independence of the motivic intervals which put him in a position to realise the unifying function of twelve-note composition even in the field of the motivic material, i.e. the smallest unit of form; the series is merely the basic shape of the work reduced to its motivic intervals. Being composed of motifs, it perforce acquires a motivic character. "Motivic" means frequent, organic repetition; one recognises a motif by its repetitions. It is an essential prerequisite for the coherence of the content of a musical form, and this alone explains why the series, which carries the motivic content of a work, must be repeated. It is only a further step to its continuous and uninterrupted repetition—though certainly a large and decisive step; the compelling musical logic of it becomes clear from the following considerations.

The series, as a de-rhythmised basic shape, presents the melodic substance of a work in, as it were, a "musically neutralised" form. From its melodic elements the music is "composed" by joining these to rhythm, which gives them shape, with rhythm's motivic elements, which are formed by the basic shape, and its non-motivic elements. But it is only the continuous ostinato-like repetition of the series which creates the necessary conditions so that the composer's powers of creative imagination can use (because of the continuous circular motion of motivic intervals which arises in this way) every detail at any moment, in every kind of variation and combination—and in any way that seems necessary to the free play of the imagination in the invention, shaping and development of musical ideas.

In this way the order of rank of the motivic intervals which is given by the basic shape—themselves moulded by the first conception of the music—can either be kept intact or varied; kept intact, or expanded by relationships caused by interval-correspondences which exist in the series, for instance, through the exchange of the positions of the note-groups, etc. This order of rank can be varied by means of a contraction of the series (see p. 119 ff.), by which notes or intervals which are placed apart in the series can be brought together in imitation of motifs or groups of motifs which have already appeared—or new motifs can be created. Or motivic intervals which are dominant in the basic shape lose this dominance, and those intervals which had previously been subordinate undertake the function of thematic "building stones". The subordinate intervals appear in an extremely diverse manner —this is a question of the musical imagination—inserted as accompaniments, subsidiary parts, figures, passage work, or chords.

It is worth noting how the series, which rotates, as it were, in musical space, takes on at each repetition a different form which is an individual one each time, and which arises from the changing motivic and thematic development. As this process demands the continuous repetition of the series, the latter thus permeates the whole organism of the work—in a way comparable to the omnipresence of tonality—unifies it and so creates the possibility of relationship to a *melodic* root in place of a harmonic or tonal one. So the law of the series expands into the higher law of musical coherence and form, as it has developed in Western music. This method of procedure in composition is preserved, in its essentials, in Schoenberg's twelve-note music also, and is merely modified to suit the purpose by exchanging the law of tonality for the law of the series.

The emancipation of the rhythmical element of the basic shape in the form of the series corresponds to that of the melodic element. The former is contained in the basic shape in two forms: as a motivic rhythm, which belongs to every individual musical motif in the basic shape; and as a rhythmical shape, taken as a whole out of the basic shape. We shall meet both forms in a very significant manner in the fourth Quartet (p. 140 ff.).

Thus we recognise the basic shape and the series as the musical centres of force, out of which the thematic material is to be invented:* invented in the form and shape which the position and function of the musical idea in question demands. For every musical shape, whether its content be simple or complicated, will not only possess its own characteristic features, but will also reveal its place in the musical organisation and its function within the work as a whole. A transitional or concluding idea will be clearly distinguishable from a main idea, and the latter will be distinguishable from a subsidiary idea which is subordinate to it; a group of main ideas will be distinguishable from a group of subsidiary ideas, such as are found in larger forms like quartets or symphonies; and an accompanying figure will be distinguishable from a subsidiary part which has acquired its own substance, as it were—the latter, again, will differentiate itself from a main part by its slower and less rich development.

Taking as a premise that the unity of musical thought and creation is natural and "given in advance", the basic features of thematic development apply to the process of musical creation as a whole, to the motif as well as to the basic shape, to the theme as well as to the form. Without regarding the possible phases in which the primary conception (basic shape) of a work develops into the most varied structures, this primary conception should always be a *total* one, i.e. it is at the same time principal and subsidiary part, accompaniment, harmony, etc. This is fundamentally a question of the concentrated "hearing out" of the original inspiration till it reaches its organic shape in full perspec-

* Ernst Krenek, in a lecture on twelve-note music given at the Free University of Berlin, in November, 1951, referred to the centuries-old practice in the development of Western music of using intervals as motivic material; these are already found in the Gregorian chorale in the form of inversions, retrogrades and retrograde inversions. He said that chorale arrangements clearly used intervals from the Canto Fermo as motivic elements in the development of the parts which play around it contrapuntally, and that Beethoven in his Quartets, Op. 132 and 131, and in the Grosse Fuge, based the whole thematic development on rising and falling steps of a second as motivic elements.

tive. In other words, in composing with twelve notes, just as before, one must work hard before the "unconscious" gives its blessing to the work.

We shall now demonstrate the invention of thematic material out of the series by examples from some of Schoenberg's works, and show its significance for the technique of composition. In general, out of (a) one series or part of it, or out of (b) two or more forms of the series simultaneously, there may arise:

> Unison themes,
> Themes accompanied by subsidiary parts or figures or chords,
> All conceivable forms of accompaniment of the kinds mentioned above, either separately or in combination,
> Contrapuntal structures,
> Passage work and similar thematically "non-obligatory" material.

In the simplest case the principal thematic part follows the course of the series. In the Petrarch Sonnet from the Serenade, Op. 24, it is the voice part:

Op. 24, 4th mvt. (♩=176)

O könnt' ich je der Rach 'an ihr ge-ne - - sen, die mich durch Blick und Re -

- de gleich zer-stö-ret, und dann zu grösserm Leid sich von mir keh-ret.

It uses the same form of the series thirteen times in succession. The necessary variation is provided by the change in the octave pitch of the notes, and further by the fact that each line of the sonnet consists of eleven syllables, so that the second line begins with the twelfth note of the series, the third with the eleventh and so on.

The main idea of the third movement of the fourth String Quartet (Table XII Q), which is played in unison, in the manner of a recitative, is invented from the O-series transposed on to C. The reprise of this (Table XIV T) gives it melodic variation by using the I-series and by changing the octave pitch of some notes. The basic shape of the work is found in its first five bars (Table VI A). The dominating motifs are (a) the minor second downwards (I), which comes three times, D—C sharp in bar I, A flat—G in bars 3–4 and, as a variant, F—E flat in bar 2, (b) the fourth upwards (II), F sharp—B, in bars 4–5. At the same time as this a subsidiary part starts in the second violin with a rhythmically marked, rising motif of a major second (III) C sharp—D sharp. This is fundamentally only an inversion of F—E flat in bar 2, i.e. it is derived from Motif I; this is made clear by the correspondence to the fourth, F sharp—B, in bar 4 with its complementary fifth, B flat—F, in bar 2. This motif, combined with the principal part as a vertical sound, produces a minor seventh (IV) which, however, is the complementary interval to I (C sharp—F sharp + F sharp—B = C sharp—B).

All the motivic intervals in the basic shape form the series and its mirror forms (Table VII B). Here the minor second appears even more dominantly. The fifth between notes 4 and 5 also contained as a complementary interval in the "fourth" motif; the major third between notes 2 and 3 and between 8 and 9 is also contained in the minor sixth, D sharp—B, in bar 5 between the principal and subsidiary parts. There the minor sixth arises from the motivic step of a major second from the minor seventh in the second violin, and, at first, also appears as a vertical sound.

The motivic rhythms are: a rhythm in minims (bar 1), a rhythm in quavers (bars 2 and 3 and a variant in 4) and the triple chords on the second, third and fourth beats of the first three bars. In addition to these rhythmical motifs, which in combination with the series form the most diverse shapes in the course of the work, the five-bar rhythmical shape of the principal part, either as a whole or in part, often has an important function as an isorhythmic basis for melodic variation through use of the different forms of the series. First, in the formation of the main theme; although the first movement does not have the form of a classical sonata movement (see p. 169 ff.), this theme, which often returns in varied forms, possesses in content and form the character of a main theme. It consists of fourteen bars, which are extended to sixteen by a cadence-like part in the second violin; this is a parallel to bars 5–6. (N.B. All the motivic relationships which we have derived above from the basic shape are of a purely musical kind, as they make up the musical content of the basic shape. The discovery and evaluation of these relations in the form of new shapes and themes, and the development of these into larger formal units, is the real process of composition. The first phase of this is the invention of thematic material for a work which the experienced composer hears with the inner ear and already sees completely before him through his powers of conception.)

The main theme is in three sections formally. The first section consists of the five-bar basic shape, lengthened to six by the subsidiary part; it also appears, repeated in a varied form, as the third section. The second section gives the necessary contrast in between: both formally, since between the two strictly formed five-bar phrases which surround it, it contains one-bar (bar 7 with up-beat) and two-bar structures (bars 8—9) quite loosely one after another; and also in content. Though it takes account of the unity of the theme by joining itself to the final section of the basic shape—motif of the fourth and the seventh—it, however, connects this to a new one-bar figure, accompanied by a new rhythmical motif in the first violin, viola and 'cello which plays an important part later on. The up-beat before bar 7 takes its rhythm from that before bar 5 and leads to the same note, B, with which the basic shape ended (link through note and rhythm). The melodic turn taken by the notes before the beat—here treated as of secondary importance—acquires greater importance in the course of the quartet in shapes of many kinds, owing to its relationship to the minor-second motif in the basic shape. The course of the principal part (marked H) in bar 7, B—E—F sharp, corresponds motivically to the F sharp—B—C sharp in bar 5. The interval of the minor seventh now also appears melodically. In bar 8 it is combined with the "up-beat" rhythm of three quavers to form a shortened repetition of bar 7, and with the fourth-motif

(D)—E flat—B flat to form a variant of (G)—F sharp—B in bar 4. (This is a model example of what is understood by "firm connection together" of motifs; the D in bar 8 is both the final note of the seventh and also the first note of the minor second, which leads to the fourth.) Thus this two-bar phrase appears to be developed from the preceding one-bar phrase, and with the fourth at the end it makes a transition to the third part of the theme, (1) through the minor second, which has the effect of a leading note, and its continuation, B flat—B natural, (2) through the correspondence with the same fourth-motif B—F sharp in bar 10, (3) through the link with the B in bars 5, 6 and 7 and (4) through the semiquaver anticipation which takes up the rhythmical motif on the third crotchet of bar 9 and so ensures the musical flow.

The varied form of the basic shape in the third section of the theme is very instructive. Melodically the variation is very considerable as in the first section the principal part was based on the O-series, but is now derived from the retrograde. As against this, rhythmically it keeps true to the basic shape, with some unimportant alterations, and is thus immediately recognisable as a repetition of it. The alterations apply less to the shortening of the rhythmical quaver motif than to the turning towards the conclusion in bar 13, where the minor-second motif takes up the rhythm of the cadential subsidary part in bars 4–5, and so prepares and strengthens the conclusive effect of the corresponding repetition of this subsidiary part in bars 14–16. One can at once recognise its character as a thematically indefinite subsidiary part with a purely cadential function.

The melodic variation of the basic shape deserves further analysis. Firstly, after the considerable variation in bar 10 of the minor-second motif of bar 1, the B flat—A in bars 12–13 clearly shows itself to be a repetition of the A flat—G (bars 3–4) and thus restores the direct melodic relationship of this section to the first section of the theme—here coming out of the R-series! Secondly, in connection with this, the motivic intervals which remained in the background in the principal part of the first section of the theme now become prominent, especially the minor sixth in bar 11, and, somewhat less, the perfect fifth in bar 12, and so acquire their corresponding function in the theme as a whole—i.e. the function corresponding to the rôle which they have to play later in the work. A discussion of this kind, which discovers all the possible musical relations in the basic shape, is necessary in order to perceive its constructional value and, with this, the possibilities which exist for the invention of thematic material out of the series. In the case of our theme, the series is first contained horizontally in the principal part of the basic shape (bars 1–5; see p. 83); but it also appears vertically in such a way that each of the four three-note groups a–b–c–d which make up the series (horizontally), together with the three-note chords beneath it, makes up the twelve-note series in the vertical dimension as well:

| (a) 1–2–3 | (b) 4–5–6 | (c) 7–8–9 | (d) 10–11–12 |
|---|---|---|---|
| (b, c, d) | (c, d, a) | (d, a, b) | (a, b, c) |
| 4  9  11 | 7  12  2 | 10  1  6 | 2  6  7 |
| 6  7  10 | 8  11  3 | 12  3  5 | 1  5  9 |
| 5  8  12 | 9  10  1 | 11  2  4 | 3  4  8 |

so that the O-series altogether appears four times in the musical space of the basic shape. This two-dimensional function of the series is an essential contribution to the unity of the musical organism—and thus to its structure—and it is a fundamental element of composition with twelve notes. The division into groups allows both a definite order in the subdivision of the notes and also a changing sequence of chords. Each chord appears three times, but is varied in each case by the change in the octave pitch of the notes.

The second section of the theme, which musically, as a contrasting middle section, is a "connected antithesis" to the first, is derived from the I-series—there is also a contrast in this. Here, too, the division into groups is maintained, naturally not in a schematic form like that shown above, but used in a varied manner (bars 7–9). The principal part shapes the series as demanded by the motivic development, i.e. the intervals of the fourth and the seventh, the latter being a complementary variant of the second-motif. And the motifs of the fourth and the seventh arise out of the change in pitch of the fifth note, E, into the higher octave (bar 7). A further change in octave pitch in bar 8 (D) brings the repetition of the seventh, while the variation in the direction of the fourth which follows (E flat—B flat) is contained in the I-series.

The third section of the theme, taking up this motif of the falling fourth, suggests the choice of the R-series, which begins with this same motif of a falling fourth. It is thus linked melodically to the middle section which has immediately preceded it, but rhythmically to the first section, the basic shape, and so it connects the two; this third section, thanks to its isorhythmic identity with the basic shape, can now be considerably varied melodically. One should note the melodic correspondences, for instance in the quavers in bars 2 and 11; in the minor-second-motif in bars 3–4 and 12–13; the quavers on the beat in bar 12 appear as a variation of the corresponding place in bar 3. One should also note the variation in the accompaniment in bar 11, where the chordal character is changed into a melodic one, and through the interval of the seventh, B flat—A, draws the musical consequences of what has gone before, the repetition of the first section of the theme does not take place schematically, but takes account of the circumstance that it has been preceded by the second section, which contained a partly new motivic content—the interval of the seventh, in fact. (This also accounts for the coupling of the two rhythmical motifs, the three quavers plus a semiquaver from bars 6–7, which are now brought together in a chordal part in bar 12.) Further, we can now see that the seventh, as part of a chord, was already present in the background from the first bar onwards in the accompanying chords; this shows the homogeneity of the vertical and horizontal dimensions.

We should now mention some possibilities of motivic correspondence and variation contained in the structure of the series (basic shape), which will be used in the invention (and later development) of the thematic material. There is the antiposition and also the linking together of the upward and downward steps of a minor second in the first four notes of the series; it arises for example in notes 6–7–9–10, leaving out note 8. The note- and interval-sequence of 3–4–5 is also found in 10–11–12, if 12 is put into the lower octave. The very frequent appearance of the transposition of the O-series starting with A flat (G sharp)—G is due to the dominant position motivically held by this step of a minor second in bars 3–4 of the basic shape. Again, the interval between notes 2 and 3 and between notes 8 and 9 is the same, a major third. And finally there is the complementary relationship of perfect fifth—perfect fourth, and of minor or major second—major or minor seventh, which is just as natural in the perspective view of the musical space as is the varying alteration of the note-groups in the basic shape.

It can be clearly seen to what a great extent these direct motivic connections (and also the indirect ones caused by splitting up the series) contribute to the unity of the musical structure; this also shows in how many varied ways the series can be used in the technique of composition.

The main theme is followed by a transitional passage (bars 17–26), which is again split up into sections. Its motivic content is as follows: bars 17–20 combine rhythmical and melodic motifs of the main theme in a semi-contrapuntal shape. This is then "liquidated" in a four-part imitative passage (bars 21–24). Bars 25–26 take up the triplet rhythm of the preceding bars; the main part, with the crotchets D—E—G—F, follows the melodic line of the beginning of the theme. In bar 27 it gives it to the accompanying subsidiary part (N), while the first violin enters with a short and capriciously syncopated new phrase, which returns again later with various functions and in different thematic connections. It is developed from a variant of the beginning of the theme, i.e. motivically from the two steps of a minor second separated by a major third.

Let us now consider in detail how the varied thematic material of these ten bars is invented out of the series, and how the musical conception—for this must always be present everywhere as a primary factor—is shaped out of it, in fact carved out of it. Bars 17–20 are invented from the I-series. The principal part in the 'cello follows it exactly; the major seventh (minor second) with which it begins is introduced by the accompaniment which starts on the up-beat (C sharp—D sharp; see also C sharp—D in bars 13–14); so is the semiquaver rhythm, which gives this four-bar phrase its rhythmical character. Note also that from bar 17 onwards a linear accompaniment in three parts is developed motivically through the repetition of two note-groups ($c_1$, $d_1$, $d_1$, $a_1$), and through simultaneous inversion of the chords on their repetition.

Bars 21–24 show the invention of passage-work out of the series. Using the three-quaver motif on the up-beat before bar 7, they now reduce the I-series in a rhythm of a similar form to its own sequence of intervals in four imitative repetitions. From bar 24 each part, as it were, pauses, in that it repeats a note-group more than once, and so the musical development comes entirely to a standstill. From the point of view of serial technique, it is interesting that this apparently free treatment is "strict" all the same, for the liquidation of the linear development always ensures that the four note-groups make up the series vertically. The musical position of these four bars more or less corresponds to the reduction of a transitional passage to scales or chords in tonal music.

The phrase in bars 27–31, and the two bars 25 and 26 which introduce it, are all developed from the I-series, both principal part and accompaniment. But the phrase on the up-beat before bar 25 (C—A flat—G) as it were falls outside the series, and seems to be an "irregular" retrograde repetition of the preceding $a_1$ note-group (second violin, bars 23–24). However we shall meet this kind of irregularity (if one wishes to call it that; for note-groups can be treated like small independent series) fairly often in this quartet, so that it can claim the right to be regarded as a "motif" and proves that it is in no way irregular, i.e. arbitrary; see Table IX bar 167, second violin; Table XIII, bars 645–6, viola; 646–7, first violin; 654, first violin; 659, viola and 'cello; and so on. Here the repetition functions as a means of connection, both musically (see viola in bar 25) and following the series. Musically this triplet up-beat becomes what Schoenberg calls the "Motif of the Accompaniment". The motivic development of the principal part and the accompaniment and the subdivision of the series fully complement one another, even when they become subsidiary parts in bar 27 and the two-part writing becomes four-part. Here triplets and a syncopated rhythm are contrasted with one another contrapuntally; the syncopated rhythm is supported by the accompanying second violin and is invented from the O-series while the subsidiary parts are invented from the I-series, with slight variations. Corresponding to this, bars 29–31 are formed from the R- and RI-series. For the motivic semiquaver up-beat in the first violin, see the 'cello part in bar 17. The minor second is also varied to become a minor ninth (bar 29, viola). The retarding triplet quaver figure which led to the entry of the principal part in bar 25 now falls steeply downwards on to the 'cello entry on C, and thus ends the episode.

Bars 116–122 (Table VIII F) show the beginning of an 18-bar cantilena (6 + 6 + 6); its three-section form arises from two repetitions, varied melodically and in sonority, of bars 116–121. (Thus, this is not a three-section ABA form.) The main and subsidiary parts in each six bars are derived from the O-, I- and R-series respectively, and the chordal accompaniment from the I or RI a fifth lower. The melodic and rhythmical motif-elements are already known to us. The minor second and, in the accompaniment, the semi-quaver rhythm from the middle section of the principal theme predominate. As regards serial technique, a new element is that the chordal accompaniment, which is one bar long and is derived from either the first or the second half of the series, is immediately repeated each time. It thus remains parallel with the O-series, each half of which takes two bars. Further, from bar 120 on, the O-series is divided by the principal and subsidiary parts into two-note groups which regularly alternate with one another. The principal part in bar 122 takes up the last note of bar 121, a connection which is both musical and serial.

Between this idea and a reprise of the main theme, which starts in bar 165, there are twenty-five bars whose static character and position remind one of an episode in a fugue (Table VIII G). Bars 153–4 and 155–6 show how a two-bar phrase—again a different type of thematic form—developed motivically from the preceding passage, together with its accompaniment, can be invented out of one series, and how elastically its musical material fits any form that is put together from motifs. Bars 157–9 (163) show a new and original method of treating the series. A three-note ostinato figure, going through all four parts, is repeated nine times and each time continues with a different one of the remaining nine notes of the series.

In Table IX H, bar 165, we can see the method of handling the series in one of the varied repetitions of the main theme, and how this repetition is treated. (It may be mentioned in passing that the wide melodic leaps and the asymmetrical formations are in no way characteristics of composition with twelve notes in itself, but of Schoenberg's own musical style, and can already be found in his early tonal works. In addition, it is especially characteristic of his style that nothing is repeated without also enhancing the musical development. The method of "developing variation", used by Beethoven and Brahms and further developed by Schoenberg, applies to the motivic and thematic elements as well as to the series, and is a basic element of Schoenberg's musical language.)

The repetition of the main theme which we are now considering varies this theme in every respect. Formally, it is lengthened to twenty bars (7 + 6 + 7); a different, more richly developed middle section is inserted which arises from a four-bar idea which has been heard meanwhile (bar 42). In place of the previous homophonic chordal accompanying structure, there is now a contrapuntal one, with imitative entries of the beginning of the theme and a contrapuntal subsidiary part, which also comes from the four-bar phrase we have mentioned (bar 42, Table VII C).

As regards the thematic invention out of the series: the interplay of the musical development with the motivic intervals in the different forms of the series shows new possibilities of treating the series almost from bar to bar.

In bar 165 the principal part and the bass (note the gradual differentiation in their development) are invented from one O-series each, and the two middle parts from the I-series a fifth lower. In bar 167 there is a repetition of the first half of the I-series and a free treatment of the second half. There is "motivic irregularity" with the note-sequence 12—11—10 in the second violin and a free distribution of the notes in the viola part, which is subordinate musically. Such a procedure would hardly occur in a leading part.

Bars 169–170: both violin parts are invented from a threefold repetition of the first half of the O-series; in bars 172–174 the second violin and viola are invented from a sixfold repetition of the second half of the O-series. The halves of the series are here treated as independent series.

In bar 172 the first violin continues the principal thematic part of the viola, which is derived from the I-series, but with the last note of the theme it goes over the end of the series; the F in bar 175 is the last note of the O-series (from the viola) and also the first note of the R-series. In the same bar the E in the 'cello is the last note of the I and the first of the RI, which appears vertically in the first half of this bar and horizontally in the second.

In bar 178 the first violin starts on A flat, joining the R and O series. There is a variation of the repetition of the basic shape by means of a contrapuntal contraction (in the Musical Space) of its first two bars to one; the second bar (cf. bar 166) appears in the second violin, split up in its motivic elements, rhythm and intervals. In the 'cello the last two notes of the RI change places, so as to become identical with the beginning of the I-series which follows (melodic flow). In bars 177–8, note the close motivic connection (fourth-minor second) between the parts; the first violin has E flat—A flat—G, second violin D sharp (E flat) —E—B, 'cello F sharp—C sharp—D, viola F sharp—F natural—B flat (bar 179).

These and the following bars, with their "spatial" dislocation of the note-groups, are extremely instructive. In bars 179–180, in the first violin, A—B flat—D—C sharp are the inversion of the beginning of the main theme (bars 1–2). Finally we should note the invention of the three-part accompanying figures in bars 179–181.

Table IX I, bars 188 ff. show a variant of Table VIII F, bars 116 ff. The principal part appears in the inversion; instead of the subsidiary part there appears, as a second contrapuntal principal part, the viola melody of bars 66 ff., while the chordal accompaniment here keeps the same semiquaver rhythm. But the whole passage starts from the second half of bar 187, a formation in three parts containing four notes each, derived from the I-series, with the beginning of the theme, B—C—E—E flat, in the second violin as the principal part. The B—C is repeated by the viola as the beginning of its cantilena, while the second violin, now accompanying, takes up the E—E flat (D sharp) and continues this motivic step of the minor second, combined with the motivic semiquaver rhythm, as the "motif of the accompaniment," together with the 'cello. As regards serial technique, it is instructive to see how these two parts, which are connected motivically, are invented from *different* forms of the series: that in the 'cello comes from the O-series of the second principal part (first violin), that in the second violin from the I-series of the cantilena. The second principal part is also developed from the minor second, which is connected in bars 190–1 with the beginning of the main theme G—A flat—C—B.

Bars 221–8 (Table X K) have a "dissolving" character, owing to the loose juxtaposition of short one- or two-bar structures. Bars 221 and 223 show the formation of passage-work out of the series; bars 224 and 225, chords; bars 226–228, figures.*

The reprise of the two-bar opening of the main theme in the

---

* The manuscript of the score contains, in the 'cello part of bar 228, F on the second semiquaver instead of F sharp, which would be correct according to the series. As there seems to be no musical reason for the change, and as this deviation is not paralleled elsewhere, one might think that this was a mistake in copying. Richard Hoffmann, who was closely associated with Schoenberg from 1947 to his death, both as a pupil and in a personal capacity, says on this point: "These remarkable irregularities in the series often occur. Schoenberg never attached great importance to putting such 'wrong' notes right, so long as no octave doublings resulted".

Coda of the first movement, bars 239–244 (Table X L) shows a new variation in the accompaniment to the principal part and, as regards serial technique, a subdivision of the notes within the note-groups which is derived from their character as "little series", and is therefore only apparently "free".

We have already seen that in twelve-note composition, in addition to the classical variation of the motivic elements, there was also a new form of variation, which was developed out of the use of the different forms of the series or their subdivisions in a fixed isorhythmic shape. This could be seen, for instance, in the third section of the principal theme, bars 10–12, where the rhythmical shape of the first section is combined with the use of a new form of the series—here the R—in a variation of this type. Bars 411–420 in the second movement (Table XI M) show another isorhythmic variation of the series of this kind; it illustrates the manifold possibilities of its use, and is quite different from the rich and sharply defined rhythmical structure of the basic shape in bars 1–5, which at once assumes its own individuality. Here, in bars 412–414, there is a five-note phrase (principal part) which is repeated three times and considerably varied melodically each time; through the quiet evenness of its quaver movement it differentiates itself from the restlessness of its surroundings, and is thus recognised by the ear as being the same phrase on each repetition, in spite of using various half-series which differ melodically. In parallel with this is the motivic coherence caused by the motif of the minor second (⌐⌐); as regards serial technique it is interesting that this comes twice in the viola part in bars 411–413 with exactly the same notes, but is derived the first time from the RI and the second time from the R, in interplay with the use of the different forms of the series—the halves of the series here being used as independent units. There is a musical and serial link between bars 414 and 415 by means of the F sharp (G flat) in the 'cello. Then the first violin and 'cello alternate in interplay round a "static" chordal group in the second violin and viola which swings between the O and I series. One should note the melodic coherence between the G flat—F in the first violin and the C sharp—D in the 'cello; they form the beginning of the series, the opening of the principal theme.

We have already discussed the rhapsodical, recitative-like idea which begins the third, Largo, movement. The six-bar period (3 + 3) in bars 630–635 (Table XII R) contains the lyrical idea B which contrasts with the rhapsodic A theme of the movement (Table XII Q, bars 614–8); this is in an ABAB form. The principal part and the three accompanying parts are derived from a sequence of four forms of the series in such a way that the accompaniment is chiefly formed out of the minor-second motif which predominates in the series ('cello, bar 631, and viola, bar 634; see also the fluid motivic connection of the various series), while the principal part uses a new combination of motifs in which the complementary interval of the major seventh dominates, also varied by a change in octave pitch to become a minor ninth (bar 632). Note the isorhythmic series-variation between antecedent and consequent in the principal part, especially the melodic variation at the beginning of the consequent, and compare bar 632, first violin (and 'cello) with bar 635. Before the varied and expanded repetition of this theme in bars 638–645, in which the demisemiquaver figure on the up-beat is developed motivically, there is a two-bar phrase which acts as a division; it does not develop, but, as it were, marks time and, corresponding to its function, contains short figures which do not require or make one expect any particular kind of continuation. In itself it is instructive from the purely formal point of view, and it also shows how one can invent out of the series material of this kind, which is "non-obligatory" thematically.

A comparison with the repetition of the lyrical six-bar phrase, which is shortened and simultaneously worked up to a climax (Table XIII, bars 655 ff.), is instructive both musically and as regards serial technique. The development becomes more complex in moving towards the climax. While in the earlier passage (bars 630 ff.) one series sufficed for the invention of the material, now two forms of the series, used simultaneously, are needed in order to provide the four instruments with thematic material.

Shortly before this, in bars 650–1, there is an interesting case of the formation of passage-work; the one-bar phrase which falls downwards is almost note for note the same in both bars, although it is derived in the first bar from the O and in the second from the RI.

The "Ode to Napoleon", Op. 41, has a completely different musical appearance, which from the point of view of the technique of composition is concerned with different tasks from those of pure chamber music. Lord Byron's poem was set by Schoenberg for string quartet (also string orchestra), piano and a speaker. Corresponding to its poetical material, it is music which suits the dramatic character of the poem in the structure and formation of the thematic ideas, but yet shows a independent musical organisation.

An instrumental introduction of twenty-five bars presents motivic material without combining it to form a basic shape. Thus at first no series can be recognised either. Bars 1, 6, 8–9, 16–19, (21) in Table XV show the basic motivic elements of both the harmonic and the melodic kind, from which the corresponding musical characters develop in the course of the piece. As can easily be seen, these basic motifs are already contained in the first phrase of the first bar in the piano part—in the motivic sequence of intervals (b) which corresponds to an arpeggiated tonal triad; in the motivic interval of the minor third (c) and its variant ($c_1$); and above all in the first chord (a). This consists of two minor thirds, separated by a perfect fourth (d). An additional motivic interval is that of the major seventh (e) between the two outside notes of the chord. In addition this chord also contains the following motivic intervals: two overlapping minor sixths (f); and, by the combination of these with the other outside note of the chord, a three-note motif results (h). All these motivic intervals (shown in Table XV B) are used in the invention of the thematic material, as the other examples show.

If we go from the notes of the minor third downwards in minor sixths (see bars 8–9), we get a six-note chord consisting of a major and a minor chord grafted together. These six notes are already contained in bar 1, with the motif $c_1$, and also form the first half of the twelve-note series of the work. Thus the first conception of the piece was chordal in form. Just as in the Piano Piece, Op. 33a, and the first of the Six Pieces for Male Chorus, Op. 35, (but here in a more instructive manner owing to the larger form), we find a surprising expansion of twelve-note composition, not least because of the introduction of tonal triads.

This *harmonic* conception of the piece becomes even more probable if we consider its series. The second half of this is merely a transposition of the first half, and the whole series is really a chain of upward and downward steps of a minor second separated by major thirds. This means that the series is relatively un-productive of melodic motif-elements. In addition each half of the series is again symmetrical, and the second section of each half (a three-note group) is the RI of the first section. As always in such a case, the inversion at the lower fifth contains the notes of the second half of the O-series in a different order. But if we compare the first half of the I with the second half of the O, we discover very considerable correspondences between them; they consist of two two-note groups which are identical, but in a dif-ferent order, and the third group contains the same notes, but in the reverse order. In fact the construction of the series on the interval of the minor second makes it uncharacteristic from the melodic point of view, but allows a considerable amount of change of position and varied combinations of the two-note groups which form it. The RI is merely a transposition of the O, and the same applies to the R in respect of the I. Thus we have only two different forms of the series instead of four, the O and the R (or the I at the lower fifth), and for the formation of chords we only have one, the O-series (for of course the R forms the same chords as the O). Altogether eight tonal triads are possible; in an arpeg-giated, melodic form these play an essential part in the work. The chords obtained from the second half of the series are only trans-positions of the first eight chords. If one reverses the order of the two halves of the series (example $B_1$), the RI-series is identical with the O, and the I at the lower fifth with the R.

This special formation of the series naturally has musical consequences. These are contained in the first conception of the work—primarily a harmonic one, which we can regard the content of bar 1 as representing. It does contain the series, but not in an unmistakable melodic form as is the case elsewhere. Even later on, when there is a linear sequence of intervals, it deviates from other serial formations by its uniformity and lack of different intervals, and also through the absence of subdivisions resulting therefrom—subdivisions which are found elsewhere in small combinations of intervals which possess internal coherence. As we have said, the melodic fertility of this series is limited, and one can say that here the series is not the *a priori* preliminary formation of the thematic material, but rather serves to vary the harmonic element; the latter contains the motivic intervals for use in free thematic combination.

Thus one can say that the thematic and melodic ideas in the work are derivations from the strongly harmonic conception of bar 1, which we can now recognise as a special and new kind of basic shape. The small number of examples in Tables XV–XVII gives a conception of the flexibility and elasticity with which these thematic combinations fit themselves to the changes in the dramatic expression and interpret it in a clear and characteristic manner. "Dramatic" in music does not merely mean crude dynamics and strongly marked rhythm (though the latter is very effectively used in this work), but the firm and direct antiposition of contrasting musical characters. In the present case this demands relatively short, flexible phrases and figures with a strong rhythmic profile. A long-drawn-out idea, even of only eight bars, for instance, would demand a length of time which the spoken poem could hardly give it. The style of this music takes account of this, and this consideration is also reflected in the special form of a series without any essential melodic obligation.

Unfortunately space does not permit us to discuss the first of the Six Pieces for Male Chorus, Op. 35, from the point of view of thematic invention from the series; for it is definitely contrapuntal music, in which the musical development is carried on, not by an idea which is thematic in itself, but by a special kind of development by means of motivic working. Thus one must have the whole piece in front of one in order to see how the contrapuntal development is completed by its own individual means out of the five-bar basic shape (Table XVII A) and the twelve-note series which is contained in it, partly vertically (Group A in both tenors), and partly in a linear manner (B and C).

The four-note groups A, B and C exchange places in the manner of double counterpoint, used sometimes vertically, sometimes horizontally, in inversion and retrograde, brought together in melodic coherence both as a whole and in their subdivisions, and subjected to augmentation and contrapuntal treatment. The twelve-note series as such only appears once, and not before bars 23–25, with both its halves treated in a double canonic stretto. Otherwise the note-groups remain extremely independent, like small series, as is suitable in the contrapuntal method of writing.

The Fantasy for Violin and Piano, Op. 47, a richly articulated work in one movement, lasting about ten minutes, shows a fundamentally different picture, both musically and as regards serial technique, from the works discussed so far. The first reason for this is that in this work, from the first bar to the last, the violin alone contains the principal part and thus the musical content. In order strictly to maintain the desired soloistic and virtuoso character of the piece, Schoenberg wrote the violin part separately first and then added the piano accompaniment. This homophonic conception of the work introduces a special element into the composer's problem and its solution.

Table XVIII A shows the three-bar basic shape and the six-bar first idea which is developed from it. A twelve-note series *can* be derived from this basic shape, but—let us say this at once—this is not the O-series of the piece, as we shall see later on, but only its first half, followed here by its inversion at the lower fifth (see p. 98). Bars 3—6 are derived from the retrograde of the first half of the O-series, the second half of which appears for the first time in bars 10 and 11. This is unusual, and possibly is connected with the new type of form shown in this work (see p. 173); the form develops from small ideas and units of form to larger and larger ones. We have already discussed in detail (p. 98 ff.) the peculiar structure of the four forms of the series.

Example C (bars 31–33) starts with the beginning of the basic shape. From the O-series, which is now present complete, a variant of the first idea, also contrasting in character, is derived; it leads into a *cantabile* of six bars, which is also derived from the O-series, this time transposed. This transposition occurred for purely musical reasons; the step of a minor second, E flat—D, the motivic interval with which this six-bar phrase began, is a contraction of the preceding E flat—F sharp—D through leaving out the quaver F sharp; this gives E flat as the first note of the transposition of the O-series.

This example shows us, in close connection with the motivic development, an entirely new method of handling the series; each phrase takes up the last notes (or sometimes motifs) of the preceding one, and carries it on further. This causes an "overlapping" in both the motifs and the series, with the effect of a far-reaching and broad melodic development.

The irregularly formed (5 + 3) eight-bar phrase in Example D shows the same kind of development with a scherzo-like idea. The difference here from Example C is that the motivic element arises not from the melody but the rhythm, and the overlapping of the groups is therefore less noticeable. The first five bars are derived from a transposed O-series, with its second half (which is handled independently) repeated; the three-bar consequent comes from a transposition of the I-series. The carefully handled quaver rhythm here has precedence over the melodic element; the phrase of five quavers can be traced back to the rhythmical motif T2 in Example A.

In Example E we see a new six-bar idea of scherzo-like character, derived from the O- and RI-series, starting from a variant Tx of the rhythmical figure in Example A. Bars 147–8 contain a clearly cadential contraction of the preceding four bars; the melodic flow of the development from the motivic content of bar 143 does not allow one to become conscious of the difference between the two forms of the series, or of the transition between them.

Examples F and G show two different thematic ideas, derived from transposed I-series. The first is a twelve-bar Lento which shows the close coherence between the reduction of the musical phrases (leading towards the end) with the (melodic) reduction of the series. The second is a recitative-like idea of a dramatic quality; it is the first section of a nineteen-bar episode which is divided into three sections. The middle section of this begins in bar 72 and consists of a variant of the three-bar basic shape.

Between the two slow sections (Examples C and G) there is a Grazioso in three sections (Example H), the first and third sections of which stem from a variant of the basic shape—the reverse of Example E; it is based on the RI, and the considerable melodic variation is compensated for by the small amount of variation in the motivic rhythm.

Entirely new phenomena occur in examples I and K. In the forty-nine-bar long scherzo-like section of the Fantasy (bars 85–133; see p. 174) the middle section, which is loosely formed and has a "dissolving" quality, contains the following passage (Example I) which is formed out of a closely interlocked complex made up of two series-forms; bars 110–112 come from the first halves of the R and RI series, first alternately using individual notes (6 and 5) from both series, then two-note groups (notes 4–3 and 2–1). Bars 113–116 consist of the second halves of the O and I series, combined together vertically.

The beginning of the Coda (Example K) shows a similar procedure; the two-part concluding idea is invented by alternate overlapping of four-note groups from the O and I series. One should note that this loose "spatial" handling of the series only appears in the later course of the piece, when the series has already "got into our ears", and that it comes in a loosely formed, "dissolving" section, to which such freedom in the handling of the series (the parallel in tonal music can be found in harmonic sequences of a modulatory character) not only corresponds, but which directly underlines its dissolutionary character.

One can easily see that the compositional procedure used by Schoenberg in his Op. 47—that of letting one phrase take up the end of the preceding one—helps both the comprehensibility and the compactness of the music. It is a motivic linking and binding, i.e. a musical process which also includes the series. Instead of the fixed note-groups which may exchange places within the Musical Space, and are handled like small independent series, we have here, as an alternative, composition with variable note-groups. These arise from the musical phrasing which binds together the smaller and the smallest units of form. They are derived from the series, and are overlapping segments of it, each of them having some notes in common with its neighbour through repetition. Thus the series permits a broader effect, a real "singing out", as it were; its flexibility in the service of the musical invention is enormously increased. The combination, too, of two forms of the series into a new melodic whole shows the possibilities of development which twelve-note composition still holds at the disposal of a real creative imagination, without making it necessary —which would happen if two different twelve-note series were used—to break the law of the series and its "tonality". (We should mention the close relationship to one another of these two forms of the series, which are united in such a complex manner in this work; the possibility and the inner logic of their synthesis probably depend on this fact).

The extremely characteristic rhythmical motifs of the work keep reappearing, either exactly as before or with slight variations, and thus increase the musical coherence, together with the melodic strengthening due to the series itself. The rôle of rhythm in the creation of form may be seen in the rhythmical analysis of the basic shape and the first six-bar idea (bars 1–6); the rhythmical sequence (3 + 3 bars) is symmetrical. Its period-like formation gives a firm basis, on the elements of which the thematic develop-ment builds in the later course of the piece—see Examples C, E, G, H, K, L—and also the 6/8 and 9/8 metres which appear later are anticipated in the triplets in bar 2. Example L shows one of the many combinations of rhythmical motifs. We have already discussed sections which are conceived in a similar manner, in which the rhythm dominates and creates the figures, as, for instance, in Example D. Bars 29–30 are based on a development of motif $R_1$ which is then liquidated and goes over into motif R in bar 31.

If one regards the work as a whole, one feels the effect of a "rhythmical tonality"—if one understands the expression "tonality" in the metaphorical sense, as an ordering principle.

Finally we shall discuss the invention of a song accompaniment, and as a model we will take the first of the Three Songs, Op. 48, for low voice. It is called "Sommermüd" (poem by Jacob Haringer) and is twenty-seven bars long (see Table XX). The principal part is naturally the voice part; corresponding to the content of the three four-line verses, it is a three-section, tenderly lyrical cantilena of 3 + 3/3 + 5/4 + 5 bars. It is remarkable that the third section, the expanded reprise of the first, is the first to be derived from the complete O and I series. Before that the series-forms used (in the voice part) consist of only eight notes, and include only two of the three four-note groups which make up a series. The missing note-group provides the material for the accompaniment, which is co-ordinated in parallel—either by itself, as with Group III in bars 1–3, or together with another group in a more compact sequence (bars 3–6 ff.). Thus here we have a simultaneous use of four-note and eight-note groups, which are treated like independent series. As in every other work by Schoenberg, these complete each other to make up the whole series, in both the horizontal and vertical dimensions; although in this song only an eight-note series is at first used for the voice part—again a new example of "freedom within the law".

The melodic flow which creative invention can obtain from such a combination of two eight-note series is shown in the first five-bar cantilena (bars 10–14). The transposition of the I-series, which joins on to the RR in bar 12, arises from the melodic correspondence of notes 7–6–5 of the RR with 5–6–7 of the I; these are joined melodically in this bar. This three-note sequence (a and $a_1$) of minor and major seconds ( = major and minor sevenths) appears three times in each series-form, twice in combination with the interval of the diminished fifth, which of necessity leads to the formation of corresponding four-note groups. The limitation of the melodic content of the series which thus arises corresponds, as we have already seen in a similar case, to a musical necessity arising out of artistic economy; the feeling for form demands the omission of everything superfluous. In the given space of so short a song only a correspondingly limited melodic content can be used. What is remarkable is the richness of inspiration with which Schoenberg makes music with these melodic and motivic elements and always knows how to invent new shapes out of them. One should look at the first three bars of the accompaniment; these are derived only from the four notes of Group III of the O-series, repeated four times—a parallel to the broader disposition of the harmony at the beginning of a tonal song. (In the course of this music-making with the four-note groups "in space", they are also introduced later in the retrograde, as independent series.) The first two crotchets of the first bar introduce the "motif of the accompaniment", out of Group III; corresponding to its subordinate position musically, this appears relatively slowly and with little variation. It is in two parts, and consists of the minor and major sevenths as the complementary intervals to those in the voice part (correspondence of the horizontal and vertical phenomena). With the further development in the next bar the left- and right-hand notes change places in the manner of double counterpoint (m and n); this is another form of variation, with the content remaining the same. One should note how much variety comes out of the four-note unit in these three bars, without altering this unit in any way; and how in the second half of bar 3 the accompaniment follows the "half-close" in the voice part. These three bars are a model for the study of the composition of an accompaniment out of four notes.

In bars 4–6 the accompaniment mirrors the intervallic content of the voice part, now enriched by the diminished fifth. Now two note-groups are used simultaneously, one in each hand; these, together with the voice part, complete the series, and in addition each is handled as an independent series. The accompaniment is now enriched with chords; the right hand leads, and seventh and second appear in new combinations. In bar 10, as third and sixth, and as second and seventh, again in a new motivic combination, these intervals comment on the voice part; by "tilting" both note-groups together the interval of the major third is introduced from the new combination of notes which arises in this way. G flat—B flat and E–C appear in the accompaniment, corresponding to G–B in the voice part. The E–C is resolved on to the motivic step of a seventh from bar 1.

Thus one can understand what is important when inventing an accompaniment of this kind: to invent—and to develop in accordance with the musical function of the accompaniment—characteristic accompaniment figures with the motivic elements in the voice or main part (i.e. the series). "Musical function" here means keeping the accompaniment in conformity with the character of the main part, or in a connected antithesis to it—but the antithesis should not be too great. This necessitates a series the note-groups of which show an interval-relation to one another, so that at any time, even in the smallest space, a motivic correspondence between the principal part and the accompaniment is possible.

The accompaniment in bars 13 and 14, with its pedal-point-like handling of the bass, its resting on the step of the second, F sharp —F, in the right hand, and the "composed" ritardando in the second half of bar 14, shows the typical musical picture of a "leading back to the reprise", which begins in bar 15. (In tonal music the fifth degree or a chord replacing it would come at this point, before the tonic which begins the reprise.) One should compare the variation in the accompaniment in bars 15 and 16 with bars 1 and 2; from the same motivic elements, especially the interval of the seventh, and the same exchange of notes between the hands, two accompaniments of a very different character have arisen in the two cases. One should note how the third O-group in the left hand in bars 16–17, varying the model of the accompaniment in bar 1, is repeated in the retrograde form.

Finally the four-bar postlude contains a one-bar Coda idea (bar 24), which joins together in four parts the leading motivic intervals of the song in a concentrated form, both harmonically and melodically. The right hand contains an antiposition of two groups from the series of a contrasting musical character; the second group, as it were, encloses the third in brackets (multi-dimensionality of the Musical Space). The double repetition of this one-bar Coda idea is combined with a "reduction" of the melodic semiquaver phrase, which is the most marked element in the Coda and thus the most suitable for the purpose of completing the "liquidation" of the piece.

We have tried to show in this chapter in what ways one can use the series for the invention of musical material with the most varied functions. *The time will come when the ability to draw thematic material from a basic set of twelve tones will be an unconditional pre-requisite for obtaining admission into the composition class of a conservatory.*[2] We have had to limit ourselves to the selection of a few examples—but characteristic and instructive ones—out of the almost immeasurable number which Schoenberg's works contain. From these we have tried to demonstrate the theoretical and technical bases of Schoenberg's Composition with Twelve Notes, and to show in what a rich and many-sided manner, and also how undogmatically, his masterly grasp of this method of composition was translated into music. *Certainly no more construction is required in twelve-note music than that demanded by what one calls "motivic working". How far, in any case, is construction disgraceful? Augmentations, diminutions, inversions and other mirror forms certainly do not reach the composer in a perfect form like dream images, especially when the other parts are contributing thematic material simultaneously with them.*[12]

An imaginative creative spirit will bring both law and freedom to fulfilment in a work of art if a conception or an idea binds both together and its emanations activate and renew them. These examples and their interpretation should be understood in this manner, as an exposition of a fragment of the depth and beauty of thought, of the imagination and skill which are contained in the music of this master; and also as an incitement for both the creative and the non-creative musician and the music-lover to follow these ideas and to go on searching. If this exploration finally leads a composer to find himself, then Schoenberg's idea has fulfilled its truest and finest task outside his compositions themselves.

## CHAPTER IX

## MUSICAL FORMS IN TWELVE-NOTE MUSIC

*Schoenberg's view of form—"Old" and new forms
in Schoenberg's works—Attempt at an analysis of the
Fantasy for Violin and Piano, Op. 47*

COMPOSITION with twelve notes, in Schoenberg's words, grew out of a necessity: namely that of replacing the two essential functions of tonality which unify the musical organism of a work and give it its form. As stated in the letter to J. M. Hauer quoted above, composition with twelve notes opens up new possibilities of the logical creation of form. Here we must remember that tonality is certainly one of the most important, but by no means the only means of creating form in music; besides and together with tonality there are melodic and rhythmical means which have a similar effect, and also repetition, arrangement in pairs, symmetry and so on.

In a work of art form is never an end in itself, but always merely a means to the end of presenting the content of the work; thus the form depends on the content and the way in which the latter is presented. Form's only premise is that the content possesses musical coherence and affinity in itself; for only that which coheres can create a form. In addition to other factors (of which the principle of repetition is one of the first and most important) it is tonality, and in non-tonal music Schoenberg's method of composition with twelve notes, which ensure the musical coherence within a work by unifying its content. In the previous chapter we discussed the methods of procedure in composition which aim at this result.

It is only on the basis of unity that that ordering of the musical content, which we call form, can arise. It appears as an arrangement of the content which, combined with the limitation, subdivision and putting into relationship of its component sections, makes it possible for us to comprehend this content and follow its presentation and development. The more completely the arrangement, i.e. the form, reflects the content, the more unmistakably do we hear this content, with our inner ear when reading the score, with our outer when it is actually realised in sound; the form, on the other hand, we hear only indirectly, through the effect made upon us by the content.

Musical form only becomes alive through its content. If the latter is simple or primitive, then so is the former. If the content is conventional, the form too will approach the conventional scheme of arrangement. Forms only become obsolete when their characteristics are not nourished and moulded by the content, but have to take their life from a poverty-stricken scheme derived from a conventional idea. Division into binary and ternary forms merely says something in general about the subdivision of the work, but nothing about the way in which the content is presented. Rondo, Sonata form, Scherzo say more to us; but they too are only types of forms, schemes of arrangement without any living powers of formation; they arise out of the different arrangements of the sections of a form on their repetition, and from the differences in the character of the music. The establishment of the fact that one movement is a rondo and another a scherzo is only a listing of certain categories of musical development. It says nothing about what is special or unique in a work—which is the sign of every real work of art—in regard to either its form or its content. Beethoven, for instance, wrote about a hundred movements in sonata form; but none of them is the same as another one, for each of them has a new and different content. It is this that makes the difference between the movements, not the type of form shown in the catalogue. And in several of Beethoven's last sonatas and quartets it would be difficult to place each movement in a definite formal scheme, even externally. True form, in both senses of the word, only begins where the formal scheme is in doubt.

As has been said: *Schemes of musical arrangement, even if they exist a priori, should only be discovered after they have been used.*[7]

Thus a handling of form which is alive and has an artistic purpose must always arise out of the content of the music in a piece, and from the structure and the needs of its musical ideas; otherwise it soon becomes formalism. But if one starts from the content and the conditions it imposes, one can quickly see that there are no "old" forms; at the most there are forms which are listed and known, but which are always capable of renewing themselves from the content—if this content arises from the spirit of a really creative person, i.e. an artist, to whom *everything he sees will become an unusual case through the way in which he sees it.*[13]

Schoenberg was never confronted with the problem of using "old" or "new" forms *a priori*: for each one of his works became an "unusual case" through its content and form. He never wrote forms, but always music. *In a real work of art it is like this: everything looks as if it had come first, because everything was born at the same time. The feeling already is the form, the thought already is the word.*[14] Whether in tonal or non-tonal or twelve-note music, the freedom and power of his feeling for form always allowed him to do what was right, i.e. what was necessary, in every case. And what was necessary, that is to say necessary for the content and its presentation, always became the unusual, without Schoenberg *willing* it to be so. In the first String Quartet, Op. 7, in D minor Schoenberg took as a model the first movement of the "Eroica"; in the first Chamber Symphony, Op. 9, the classical movement-forms are reshaped in a way which is both surprising and convincing; classical forms appear in twelve-note works like the Wind Quintet, Op. 26, or the two instrumental concertos—but in all these cases each work has its own unchangeable and individual appearance—that, in fact, which the content of the music gives it. It is immaterial whether these forms, or their subdivisions and limits, are arrived at by tonal or twelve-note means; this depends only on the structural constitution of the ideas in them. Composition with twelve notes can, but need not, lead to new forms; this entirely depends on the content. One would naturally expect that the "possibilities of the logical creation of form" which this method produces would also cause the appearance of new forms; but to make this a *requirement*, and to regard the capability of creating new forms as a criterion of the worth or worthlessness of this method of composition only shows complete misunderstanding of the idea and essence of the method. And it shows mistaken thought; for forms could never arise from a technique of composition—they only arise from ideas.

In fact we find in some of Schoenberg's works, composed over a period of about twenty-five years, new, "free" forms as well as "old" ones, either within a work or shaping a work as a whole— forms which are only vaguely similar to those we have known up to now. These defy formal analysis of a traditional kind. Examples are, the first and second movements of the third String Quartet and the first and last movements of the fourth String Quartet, the String Trio, Op. 45, and the Fantasy for Violin and Piano, Op. 47. These are new, free forms, which were not consciously worked out in advance, but, like the old forms, grew out of the music itself, through the innate laws of logical coherence, clarity and comprehensibility. It is clear that this unpreconceived and unmethodical approach of Schoenberg to the creation of form puts special difficulties in the way of analysis—even of those movements which correspond to forms which are already known; for his approach was based not on a *willed* form, but on a sense of form which makes willing unnecessary, that is to say, on his unerring confidence in the logic of his own musical thinking. The form simply follows the needs of the content of the work, and is therefore as "unusual" as the content itself. Musical theory is still far behind what actually happens in music. *Fluent coherence and logic in music arise from factors which have not yet been unmistakably defined. In the older styles repetitions, variations, transformations, etc., of the fundamental elements created aural and visual coherences and, supported by subdivisions, they marked out the extent and content of a work, following the demands of comprehensibility. In spite of this all these old master have also written preludes, introductions, fantasies, toccatas, fugues and many similar compositions in which they allowed their powers of imagination free and unlimited scope; in doing this they renounced the use of almost all the formal and articulating means which provided the form in others of their works.*

*In fact musical theory has not yet attempted to uncover many of these factors, which are the functional attendants of the motifs, their derivations and coherences. In my book "Structural Functions of Harmony" I have criticised this fact and have at least given such harmonic foundations on which "free forms" can be based. And that is all that we know up to now.*[15]

The study and description of the forms in Schoenberg's works thus demand a complete and fundamental re-examination of the concept of musical form,* In the analyses of his four Quartets Schoenberg confines himself to mentioning new movement-forms in the third and fourth Quartets and gives some clues which could help in the analysis of them. Concerning the first movement of the third Quartet he states: *In this first movement there is a "shape" which is almost always present and which can be regarded as a unifying connective for all the more remotely related characters and moods.* (See p. 89.)

*The notes, intervals and rhythm of this figure undergo countless alterations, often only for the sake of variation or because of a change of mood or character, or because additional counter-parts so wish it; but also in order to produce as many contrasts as the situation demands. The metre is usually preserved by the fact that eight quavers appear in a group. But, especially through changes in tempo—ritardando, ruhiger, Tempo I etc.—these are reduced to a smaller number, or, on the other hand, expanded. These groups appear mainly as an accompaniment to a leading part. But they are also combined to form transitions, connections, subordinate themes and short episodes.*[15]

This clearly indicates the function of the rhythmical element in creating form, which has been discussed several times in the preceding chapters.

* A fundamental enquiry of this kind has been undertaken by Erwin Ratz in his *Einführung in die Musikalische Formenlehre,* with regard to the formal principles in J. S. Bach's Inventions and their importance for Beethoven's technique of composition (published by Osterreichischer Bundesverlag, Vienna, 1951).

Following Schoenberg's indications, one could perhaps regard the second movement of the same quartet as a combination of a variation movement and a Rondo form. None of the repetitions of the main theme and its variants appears without alteration. On the other hand, the musical character of the individual variations, as well as their complementary relations to one another, clearly obey a definite law of form, which often demands far-reaching structural changes which are foreign to the strict classical variation form. Here, too, a good many of the formal relationships can be explained by the rhythmical element.

In the fourth Quartet, like the third, the first movement is greatly dominated by rhythmical motifs, which play a part in its formal subdivision. We have already seen what an essential part these play, combined in the form of the "basic shape", in the three-sectional formation of the main theme, in order to give a coherent effect. We find the quaver rhythm of the basic shape, and the three-beat rhythm of the chords which accompany it, acting as motivic elements in the musical development; they cause the appearance of new figures, and ensure the coherence of the larger formal sections by providing a rhythmical basis and producing musical contrast between the different sections.

In this connection we should mention once again the way in which rhythm's formative powers are combined and inter-locked with those of the twelve-note series; they augment each other in alternation in order to prepare the ground on which the form arises.

In these new forms we can recognise a characteristic feature—the absence of long "working-out" sections, such as are found in the classical sonata-form movement and scherzo. The formal function of the classical "working-out" section was to create as sharp a contrast as possible to the sections on each side of it; and also a difference in structure, which applied to all the elements of form. In contrast to the relatively "fixed" form of the sections on each side of it, the "dissolving" character of the working-out section is reflected in the rapid and frequently changing modulatory progressions of the harmony, and in the tendency towards formations consisting of a small number of bars, as well as in the loose juxtaposition of these—and also of contrasting musical ideas—to one another. On the other hand, with Schoenberg the new forms show a clear tendency, both in form and character, towards "fixed" musical ideas which are moulded in a definite shape. One might mention that the inner logic of the development of this great master is again shown by the fact that as early as 1919 he described the working-out section to his pupils as a formal section which gave the opportunity of *new invention*. But for him this "invention" always meant the invention of *shapes*. Clarity of thought was an absolute and natural law for him; and he felt that the clear expression of a musical idea could only be achieved by means of a definite shape. "Developing variation" was an essential means of producing shapes by permitting multiplicity to arise from unity (i.e. from a basic idea or basic shape), and also of ensuring coherence and logic—and thus form too—within a whole. Here is an example of how far back this goes, and how characteristic it is of Schoenberg's conception of music and his method of thought. In the analysis of his four quartets mentioned above he says that his aversion to the traditional working-out section made him either reduce or leave out altogether the working-out sections in the first two movements, a sonata-form movement and a scherzo, of his second String Quartet, composed in 1907–8. Instead he made the third movement, a setting of Stefan George's "Litanei", the "working-out" of the content of the two first movements. What is new and surprising is that this is done in the strict classical variation form—in this case, a theme with five variations and a postlude; i.e. in a form which consists of the juxtaposition of several shapes which are developed out of one idea. (He had another reason, too, for choosing the variation form; its strict balance was to act as a counterweight to the strongly emotional content of the poem and avoid dramatic exaggeration.)

Instead of the working-out section, the thematic or episodic shape seems to appear in Schoenberg's new forms in order to provide musical contrast on a large scale (the score of the String

Trio, Op. 45, contains the indications: First and Second Episode). In this the contrast naturally applies not only to the musical character, but also to the countless types of formal creation which can arise from a shape of this kind.

Because of its relatively short length of 166 bars and its "one-part" structure, the Fantasy for Violin and Piano, Op. 47, is specially suited to illustrate the development of one of these new forms, its "shape-elements" and the way in which these are combined to form a whole.

However new a form may be, in order to be valid as a form it must present two factors—limitation (i.e. coming to a conclusion) and subdivision. In Op. 47 both are clearly and unmistakably present.

The "limitation", which in a work of art means not just stopping but reaching a conclusion, is shown in the Coda, bars 136–166. This consists of two sections: (a) the actual seven-bar Coda-idea, with its repetition and a reduced form of it (bars 136–153), and (b) a short varied repetition, enlarged to six bars, of the basic shape of the work; this leads to a virtuoso cadenza of seven bars, with which it closes.

As regards subdivision, there is a marked caesura in the middle of the work, at bar 85. This arises both from the contrast in the basic musical character and from the formation of the two sections. The second section, from bar 85 to the Coda, has a unified scherzo-like character in a definite three-section form, ABA. The A is a sixteen-bar period consisting of two irregular (5 + 3) eight-bar phrases; in its reprise this is expanded to seventeen bars by lengthening the last bar. B also consists of sixteen bars, but, in contrast to A, is relatively loosely constructed; it is made up of an eight-bar and a six-bar phrase. The former resolves into a semiquaver rhythm (bars 109–110) which simultaneously introduces the six-bar phrase which follows (also containing semiquavers), while the rhythmical shape of the latter prepares for the Coda-idea. Similarly, bars 100–101 lead from the two-beat 6/8 metre to the three-beat metre with which the eight-bar phrase begins; but this 3/4 bar has already been anticipated in bar 87. Rhythmical correspondences and transformations of this kind ensure both the flow and the coherence of the music and can be found everywhere in this work. Where ideas have to be separated or else connected, one or two—at the most three—bars are enough for Schoenberg; these act so to speak as a comma, semicolon or end of paragraph.

In natural contrast to the second section, which is going "to rest", i.e. towards a conclusion, bars 1–84 are much richer in changing contrasts. They form a chain of shorter and longer shapes, the more or less immediate antiposition of which gives this first section—in contrast to the gay second section—a character which is full of tension and predominantly dramatic. Its formal coherence, like that of the second section, arises from the common derivation and development of the various shapes out of the basic shape.

Formal Analysis

| | Bars | | Thematic Shapes |
|---|---|---|---|
| | 1— 24 | (Grave) : | $(6\,(3+3)+3)+4+$ $(4+7)$ |
| | 25— 33 | (Piu mosso) | $4+2+3$ |
| | 34— 39 | (Lento) | $3+3$ |
| | 40— 51 | (Cantabile) | $5+5+2$ |
| | 52— 62 | (Grazioso) | $4+4+3$ |
| | 63 | | Connection |
| $ABA_1$ | 64— 81 | (Grave) | $8\,(5+3)+4+6\,(4+2)$ |
| | 82— 84 | | Connection |
| A (Scherzando) | 85—100 | | $8+8$ |
| | 100—101 | | Connection |
| B | 102—109 | | 8 |
| | 110 | | "Liquidating" connection |
| | 111—116 | | 6 |
| A | 117—133 | | $8+9$ |
| | 134—135 | | Connection |
| Coda (a) | 136—153 | | $7+7+4$ |
| (b) | 154—166 | | $4+2+7$ |

If one looks at the work as a whole, one may perhaps characterise its formal development by saying that longer and longer units of form and shape keep arising out of the three-bar basic shape. The more one studies the work, the more one can find surprising musical relations of a new sort which arise from correspondences and similarities of both rhythmical and melodic types: for instance, if one compares bars 56–58 and 82–84 with bars 7–9, or bar 34 with bar 55, and bars 37–38 with bars 58–59. Bar 69 of the *Grave* idea (bars 64–81) prepares for the middle section (bars 72–75), which is then heard again in a contracted form in the characteristic motivic seventh intervals of bars 82–84). The derivation of the middle section itself from the basic shape is clear to see; but the very ingeniously concealed lead-back to the reprise $A_1$, is less easy to analyse. The second half of bar 75, and bar 76, take up bars 69–71, note for note. Bars 78–79 should also be compared with bars 66–68; the formal correspondences here are based on the series of the work.

We have come to the end of what can be said here about Schoenberg's Method of Composition with Twelve Notes. The extent to which the creative work of this master can be felt as the beginning of a new epoch in music—though it cannot yet be viewed as a whole and can only be partly comprehended—and the way in which from year to year the recognition is growing that it shows a path which is sure, universally valid, and open to everyone in his own way, and which leads us out of the mass of confusing possibilities—all this is attested and demonstrated in the next section by composers of all generations and countries, each in his own manner. But, as always when one speaks about art, and especially about music, there is left an unresolved remainder which defies all theory and all rational comprehension and definition. In his essay *Das Schicksal der modernen Kunst* (Cornelsen Verlag, Berlin) Wladimir Weidlé quotes a remarkable phrase from a letter of John Keats, written in 1817. Keats speaks there of the "negative capability" of the artist, which Shakespeare, for instance, "possessed so enormously". And Weidlé calls this negative capability the positive gift of the true artist of completely trusting the logic of his intuition against all the considerations of reason—the gift of seeing the "mystery of things", the "miraculous", which logical reason cannot approach; the unconscious which speaks to us from every true work of art and constitutes its true and deepest essence. Because—to repeat a saying of Schoenberg's—what happens unconsciously is always more than what we can achieve by conscious thought.

## Arnold Schoenberg: Sketch for a Series of Lectures for a Twelve-Week Course of Three Two-Hour Lessons a Week*

THE topics listed here will demand more than one day's class in many cases. They will be illustrated with examples from musical literature; a projector will probably be necessary for this. The order given here is not compulsory.

I *Construction of the first section of a sonata, quartet movement, symphony, etc.*

    1  What is necessary for thematic material

    2  Characteristics of the themes with reference to their position and importance

    3  Motivic coherence of themes

    4  The use of harmony

    5  Means of providing the necessary contrasts, and a fluid course of the presentation of the ideas

    6  The technique of transition

    7  Provision of various kinds of cadence

    8  The technique of liquidation

II *The "Durchführung"†, the contrasting middle section*

    1  The fundamental difference in construction of the component elements

    2  The modulatory course of the harmony, its way and purpose

* Placed at the author's disposal in 1949.
† See note on p. 11.

3   "Working-out" of a single theme

4   "Working-out" of several themes
    (a) In loose sequence
    (b) In contrapuntal or polyphonic combination

5   Ways of connecting or contrasting the individual sections
    (a) Linking by transitions
    (b) Separation from one another by liquidation
    (c) Juxtaposition in contrast

6   The lead-back and preparation for the Reprise
    (a) Simple "leading over" as in Mozart
    (b) Working up of dramatic tension as in Beethoven

III   *The Reprise; alterations which are necessary and those which are not*

1   The tonal position of the subsidiary group

2   The "fateful" alterations in the main theme and on occasion in the subsidiary theme too

3   The alterations in the writing or instrumentation in spite of unaltered character and expression

4   Smaller variants and variations in minor matters

IV   *The Coda*

1   Shorter final sections consist of
    (a) Several shorter cadential units
    (b) Several modulations which quickly return, using fragments of motifs
    (c) Liquidation-like reduction of such units leads back to the tonic

2   Longer and more independent Codas consist of several groups of this kind, which are also in harmonic contrast with one another. The actual ending is then introduced in a way similar to that described in the shorter Coda in (1) above. A certain similarity to the *Durchführung* is often discernible.

### THE TECHNIQUE OF VARIATION

1 Illustrated by Beethoven's C minor and Diabelli Variations and Brahms' Variations on a Theme by Haydn (these analyses will need at least 3–4 classes)

2 The use of variation technique in other works

3 The technique of developing variation

Analyses of a number of my own works on the foundation of the theoretical basis set out above. (These will be chamber and orchestral works from most important stylistic periods.)

| | |
|---|---|
| 1897 | String Quartet in D major |
| 1897 (98?) | Two Songs, Op. 1 |
| 1899 | Four Songs, Op. 2 |
| 1899 | String Sextet, Op. 4 |
| 1899–1903 | Six Songs, Op. 3 |
| 1900–1911 | 'Gurrelieder' |
| 1903 | Symphonic Poem "Pelleas und Melisande", Op. 5 |
| 1903–1905 | Eight Songs, Op. 6 |
| 1904 | Six Orchestral Songs, Op. 8 |
| 1905 | First String Quartet in D minor, Op. 7 |
| 1906 | First Chamber Symphony in E major, Op. 9 |
| 1907 | Two Ballads for voice and piano, Op. 12 |
| 1907 | "Friede auf Erden", mixed chorus a cappella, Op. 13 |
| 1907–1908 | Second String Quartet in F sharp minor, Op. 10 |
| 1907–1908 | Two Songs, Op. 14 |
| 1908–1909 | Fifteen Songs after Stefan George, Op. 15 |
| 1909 | Three Piano Pieces, Op. 11 |
| 1909 | Five Orchestral Pieces, Op. 16 |
| 1909 | "Erwartung", monodrama, Op. 17 |
| 1910 | Three small pieces without title for several instruments (the third uncompleted) |
| 1911 | Six Little Piano Pieces, Op. 19 |
| 1911 | "Herzgewächse", Op. 20 |
| 1912 | "Pierrot lunaire", Op. 21 |
| (1908)–1913 | "Die glückliche Hand", drama with music, Op. 18 |
| 1913–1916 | Four Orchestral Songs, Op. 22 |
| 1917 (–1922) | "Die Jakobsleiter", oratorio |
| 1920–1923 | Five Piano Pieces, Op. 23 |
| 1920–1923 | Serenade, Op. 24 |
| 1921 | Suite for Piano, Op. 25 |

| | |
|---|---|
| 1922 | Song of the Wood-Dove from "Gurrelieder", for chamber orchestra |
| 1922 | J. S. Bach, Two Chorale Preludes, arranged for orchestra |
| 1923–1924 | Quintet for Winds, Op. 26 |
| 1924–1926 | Suite (Septet) for piano, 3 winds and 3 strings, Op. 29 |
| 1925 | Johann Strauss, Emperor Waltz, arranged for chamber ensemble |
| 1925 | Four Pieces for Mixed Chorus ,Op. 27 |
| 1925 | Three Satires for Mixed Chorus, Op. 28 |
| 1925–1926 | Appendix to Op. 28 |
| 1926–1928 | Variations for Orchestra, Op. 31 |
| 1927 | Third String Quartet, Op. 30 |
| 1928 | J. S. Bach, Prelude and Fugue in E flat major, arranged for orchestra |
| 1928 | Piano Piece, Op. 33a |
| 1928 | Three German Folksongs (15th and 16th centuries), arranged for mixed chorus a cappella |
| 1928–1929 (Jan. 1) | "Von Heute auf Morgen", opera, Op. 32 |
| 1929 | Four German Folksongs (15th and 16th centuries), arranged for voice and piano |
| 1929–1930 | Accompaniment to a Film-Scene, Op. 34 |
| 1929–1930 | Six Pieces for Male Chorus, Op. 35 |
| 1931 | Piano Piece, Op. 33b |
| 1930–1932 | "Moses und Aron", opera |
| 1932–1933 (Jan. 4) | Concerto for 'Cello and Orchestra, after the harpsichord concerto of G. M. Monn |
| 1933 | Three Songs, Op. 48 |
| 1933 | Concerto for String Quartet and Orchestra (after Handel) |
| 1934 | Suite for String Orchestra |
| 1934–1936 | Violin Concerto, Op. 36 |
| 1935 | First Chamber Symphony, arranged for orchestra, Op. 9B |
| 1936 | Fourth String Quartet, Op. 37 |

| 1937 | Brahms, Piano Quartet in G minor, arranged for orchestra |
| 1938 | "Kol nidre", for speaker, mixed chorus and orchestra, Op. 39 |
| 1939 | Second Chamber Symphony, Op. 38 (begun 1906) |
| 1941 | Variations for Organ, Op. 40 |
| 1942 | Ode to Napoleon, for speaker, piano and string quartet, Op. 41 |
| 1942 | Concerto for Piano and Orchestra, Op. 42 |
| 1943 | Theme and Variations for Band, Op. 43A; version for orchestra, Op. 43B |
| 1945 | Prelude for Orchestra and Mixed Chorus, Op. 44 |
| 1946 | String Trio, Op. 45 |
| 1947 | A Survivor from Warsaw, for speaker, male chorus and orchestra, Op. 46 |
| 1948 | Three Folksongs for mixed chorus a cappella, Op. 49 |
| 1949 | Phantasy for Violin with Piano Accompaniment, Op. 47 |
| 1949 | "Dreimal tausend Jahre", for mixed chorus a cappella, Op. 50A |
| 1950 | "De Profundis", Psalm 130, for mixed chorus a cappella, Op. 50B |
| 1950 | Modern Psalm (text by the composer), for mixed chorus, speaker and orchestra, Op. 50C |
| 1950–51 | Thirty canons |

Undated, and therefore not included in this list, are the orchestration of Carl Löwe's "Der Nock" and the realization of the continuo of the works by G. M. Monn and J. C. Mann, which were probably done about 1910 or 1911.

# Arnold Schoenberg. Wind Quintet. Op.26.

2nd Movement.

(Cont. over page)

XII

4th Movement

Arnold Schönberg, Ode op. 47

Arnold Schönberg
6 Pieces for
Male Chorus
Op. 35. No. 1

Ist ih - - nen die Spra - - - che_ ver-sagt_ ?

Ist ih - - nen die Spra - - - che_ ver-sagt_ ?

Ist ih - nen die Spra - che ver- sagt_ ?

Ist ihnen die Sprache ver-sagt_ ?

Und sie re - den doch so flüs - sig, wenn sie ei - ne Ab - sicht

Und sie re - den doch so flüs - sig, wenn sie ei - ne

Und sie re - den doch so flüs - sig, wenn sie

Und sie re - den doch so flüs - sig, wenn sie ei - ne Ab - sicht ha - ben;

Arnold Schönberg, Fantasy for Violin and Piano, Op. 47

XX

Arnold Schönberg, "Sommermüd" from 3 Songs, Op. 48.

Wenn du schon glaubst, es ist e - wi - ge Nacht,

hat dir plötzlich ein A - bend wie - der Küsse Sf und Sterne gebracht.

wird auf ein - - - mal wie - - - der Christ - - -

- - nacht und lieb - - - - - - - - - li - cher

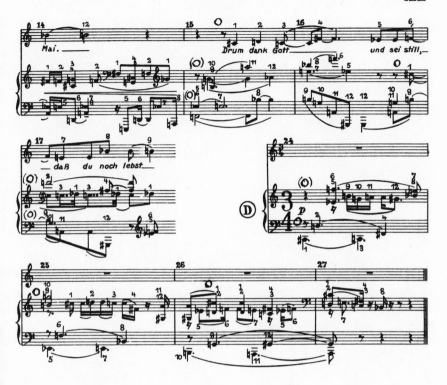

# LIST OF SOURCES

(1) Letter of 25 July, 1949, to the author
(2) Schoenberg, "Composition with Twelve Tones", (*Style and Idea*, Philosophical Library, New York, 1950)
(3) Letter of 7 December, 1923, to J. M. Hauer
(4) Aphorism (?)
(5) "Heart and Brain in Music" (*Style and Idea*)
(6) Oral
(7) Arnold Schoenberg, "Zur Kompositionslehre" (*Die Musik*, May, 1931, Max Hesses Verlag, Berlin)
(8) Letter to J. M. Hauer of 1 December, 1923
(9) Letter of 5 February, 1951, to the author
(10) Letter of 8 April, 1950, to the author
(11) Schoenberg, "Rückblick", in *Stimmen*, No. 16 (H. Knauer, Berlin, 1949)
(12) Letter to the author, 1950 or 1951
(13) Schoenberg, "Problems of Artistic Education"
(14) Merle Armitage, "Arnold Schoenberg"
(15) Schoenberg, "Analyses of the Four String Quartets"

## Acknowledgments

Thanks are due to the following publishers for permission to reprint the musical examples:

Universal Edition, Vienna
> Three Piano Pieces, Op. 11
> Suite for Piano, Op. 25
> Wind Quintet, Op. 26
> Third String Quartet, Op. 30
> Variations for Orchestra, Op. 31
> Piano Piece, Op. 33a

G. Schirmer Inc., New York
> Fourth String Quartet, Op. 37
> Ode to Napoleon, Op. 41

Wilhelm Hansen, Copenhagen
> Five Piano Pieces, Op. 23
> Serenade, Op. 24

Peters Edition, New York—London—Frankfurt
> Fantasy for Violin, Op. 47

Bote & Bock, Berlin
> Six Pieces for Male Chorus, Op. 35

Bomart Music Publications Inc., Hillsdale, N.Y.
> Three Songs, Op. 48

# INDEX

Arnim, Bettina von, 6

Bach, 11, 37–8, 52, 53n, 82, 86–7, 127, 170n, 192
  Art of Fugue, 11, 38, 82
  Musical Offering, 11, 38, 82
  Three-Part Invention No. 9, 86–7
  Well-Tempered Clavier, 11
Balzac, 8
Bartók, String Quartet No. 1, 20
Beethoven, 3, 6–7, 24, 27–9, 35, 38–44, 60, 63, 65, 82, 92, 136, 139, 139n, 149, 167, 170n
  Grosse Fuge, 139n
  Piano Sonata, Op. 2 No. 1, 17, 28
  Piano Sonata, Op. 2 No. 2, 35
  Piano Sonata, Op. 2 No. 3, 28, 32, 35
  Piano Sonata, Op. 7, 35
  Piano Sonata, Op. 10 No. 1, 28–9, 35, 38–44, 60, 92, 136, Tables I & II
  Piano Sonata, Op. 10 No. 2, 30
  Piano Sonata, Op. 13, 35
  Piano Sonata, Op. 14 No. 1, 33
  Piano Sonata, Op. 14 No. 2, 35
  Piano Sonata, Op. 28, 35
  String Quartet in C sharp minor, Op. 131, 7, 139n
  String Quartet in A minor, Op. 132, 139n
  String Quartet in F major, Op. 135, 12, 63
  Symphony No. 5, 27
Benn, Gottfried, 9
Berg, Alban, 20, 64, 104–5
  Chamber Concerto, 64, 105
  Lulu, 104
  Violin Concerto, 104
  Wozzeck, 20
Blacher, Boris, 132n
Brahms, 3, 29–30, 49–50, 52, 53n, 82, 86–7, 127, 170n, 192
  Piano Quartet in A minor, 30
  Variations on a theme of Handel, 49–50, 72
  Variations on a theme of Paganini, 29
Bruckner, 3

Debussy, 16

Goethe, 6, 15n
Gurlitt, Willibald, 11

Hába, Alois, 105
Haringer, Jakob, 161
Hauer, J. M., 77, 166
Haydn, 36
Hesse, Hermann, 8–9
Hindemith, 19–20
  Cardillac, 19
  String Quartet No. 3, 20
  String Trio No. 2, 19
Hoffmann, Richard, 151n

Kant, 4
Keats, 175
Krenek, Ernst, 139n

Leibowitz, René, 106

Luigi, Table XXIV

Mendelssohn, 3
Mozart, 31, 36

Nietzsche, 9

Pückler-Muskau, Prince Hermann von, 6

Ratz, Erwin, 170n
Reger, 3, 18
  String Quartet in F sharp minor, Op. 121, 18
  String Trio, Op. 141b, 19
  Violin Sonata, Op. 122, 18

Schoenberg:
  Books:
    *Harmonielehre*, 46, 48, 90
    *Models for Beginners in Composition*,
      57*n*
    *Structural Functions of Harmony*, 11*n*,
      170
    *Style and Idea*, 4–5, 8, 13, 47, 49, 51,
      63, 81, 83, 90, 96–7, 117, 120, 164
  Works:
    Chamber Symphony No. 1, Op. 9,
      168
    Fantasy for violin and piano, Op. 47,
      98–100, 108, 114, 128, 157–161,
      169, 173–5, Tables XVIII A–
      XIX K
    Jakobsleiter, Die, 22*n*
    Male Voice Choruses, Op. 35, 93,
      155–7, Table XVII A
    Moses and Aaron, 108
    Ode to Napoleon, Op. 41, 90–1, 93,
      102, 103–4, 126, 131, 133, 154–6,
      Tables XV–XVII
    Piano Concerto, Op. 42, 168
    Piano Pieces, Op. 11, 58–9
    Piano Pieces, Op. 19, 59–60
    Piano Pieces, Op. 23, 55–6, 61, 71–7,
      101
    Piano Piece, Op. 33*a*, 93, 155
    Serenade, Op. 24, 55–6, 61–70, 76–7,
      117, 140
    Songs, Op. 48, 161–4, Tables XX A–
      XXI D
    String Quartet No. 1, Op. 7, 168
    String Quartet No. 2, Op. 10, 172
    String Quartet No. 3, Op. 30, 89–91,
      169, 170
    String Quartet No. 4, Op. 37, 83–4,
      86–8, 95–6, 116–121, 124–6,
      129–130, 133–4, 138, 140–154,
      169–171, Tables VI A–XIV
    String Trio, Op. 45, 169, 173
    Suite for Piano, Op. 25, 55, 88, 91,
      97–8, 100, 123–4, Tables VI A¹ &
      B¹
    Variations for Orchestra, Op. 31, 82,
      92, 93–4, 97, 98
    Variations for Orchestra, Op. 43*b*,
      107
    Variations on a Recitative for Organ,
      Op. 40, 107
    Violin Concerto, Op. 36, 168
    Von Heute auf Morgen, Op. 32
    Wind Quintet, Op. 26, 97, 116–7
      123–4, 129, 168, Tables III–V
Schubert, 3, 192
Schumann, 3
Shakespeare, 175
Slonimsky, Nicolas, 22*n*
Strauss, Richard, 17–8, 57*n*, 92
  Also sprach Zarathustra, 17
  Arabella, 18
  Elektra, 17
  Salome, 17
Stravinsky, 93
Stuckenschmidt, H. H., 109

Webern, 20
Weidlé, Wladimir, 175

Zelter, 15*n*